BOY, WE HAD SOME GOOD TIMES: STORIES OF OUR LIVES

C. R. AND BEVERLY LAYTON

LaytonMcMahon Publications
Cleveland
2016

Copyright © 2016 C. R. and Beverly Layton

Edited by Melody Layton McMahon

ISBN-13: 978-1535327664

LaytonMcMahon Publications
Cleveland, OH
mlmcmahon@gmail.com

Contents

Grandpa's Stories

THE GREAT DEPRESSION 1929-1942	1
THE RATTLER	7
A SHORT STORY ON SHOES	8
MY SCHOOL DAYS	10
HOBOS, TRAMPS, or BUMS	12
THE OLD BOX	13
HUNTING	15
GRANDMA DOSHIE	17
GRAMPA WALT	21
WESTERN UNION	26
MY FIRST AUTOMOBILES	28
A SHORT STORY ABOUT GEORGE	33
MY GUITARS	37
BOOT CAMP	40
CARL	45
AZORES	50
MY FIRST CRUISE	55
SURVIVAL TRAINING	57
OUR OLD 750 MAN BARRACK	60
ALASKA IN THE COLD WAR	64
LOON AND PTARMIGAN	67
LIVE AMMO	69
THINGS WE REMEMBER ABOUT ALASKA	71
AN UNFORGOTTEN DAY	72
DOWN THE ALCAN HIGHWAY	77
33rd AIR DIVISION TINKER AFB, OKLA CITY, OK	82
WB-29 # 214	86
MY JOB CHAPTER 1	88

MY JOB CHAPTER 2 94
BASS FISHING 97
THE BEST CHRISTMAS GIFT 102
BUILDING OUR HOUSE 103
LAYTON CAMPING TRIPS 107
OUR FAMILY VACATION TO THE CLINCH MOUNTAINS 110
THE FUN YEARS 116
A VERY UNUSUAL GIFT 122

Grandma's Stories

REMEMBERING MY EARLY YEARS OF THE LATE 1930s & 1940s ... 125
MOTHER WAS A LADY 128
MY DAD 132
UNCLE JOHN WALKER ROGERS 134
REMEMBERING THE GOOD OLD DAYS 137
GRANNY BALDWIN 139
MY VERSION OF *THE VIEW FROM THE FOLDING CHAIRS* 141
THE OLD HOUSE I GREW UP IN 145
CLANG, CLANG, CLANG WENT THE TROLLEY 147
MY DAYS AT MARK TWAIN ELEMENTRY SCHOOL 151
THE PIANO 154
CHRISTMAS MEMORIES 155
CHRISTMAS TREES 158
TULSA GOSPELAIRES 160
THE WATERMELON STAND 163
THE WAY AND TIME I MET MY HUSBAND 164
EXPECTING OUR FIRST CHILD 165
THIS OLD HOUSE 166
RAISING OUR CHILDREN 170
HOME ROOM MOTHERS 173
A CHILD'S FAITH 174

iv

PREFACE

In late 2000, Beverly and I saw an ad in the *Tulsa World* newspaper about a beginner writer's class. It was to be at a Presbyterian Church over in Brookside on South Peoria. We discussed it and decided it might be fun so we went to the first meeting. It was led by a lady named Beth Parks. Her husband was Russ Parks, a corporate pilot for Parker Drilling here in Tulsa. Russ and I became very good friends, both being ex-military.

There were probably about twenty people there as she explained what the class was all about. It was to start at our earliest memories in life and we were to write them down into a short story and to go from there in ten year segments. Beverly and I, along with about six more, signed up for the class. We had the first couple of meetings at that church then the group decided it would be more fun to meet in a member's home and alternate it every month. We also decided to add tea or coffee and even maybe a cookie. We called our group Writers Recall Story Reading Club. Our purpose was to share ideas, motivate writing, and appreciate each other's lives. One of the most important aims was to create a value to descendants through family history. Our audience and critics were our peers in our writers' group. This gave a bunch of retirees something to do and was also great fellowship. As the group progressed it changed. Every once in a while someone would join in and some might drop out. We met a lot of really good people and enjoyed their company very much. The group met for a few years.

After that, I continued to write stories for the Air Force Reunion book I made every year. Beverly didn't write much until Melody had the idea for this book. At first, Beverly didn't think she had anything else to write about, but when she started she found she had a bunch of stories to write. Then Melody started asking us to write about certain events or people. It was a lot of fun to remember these things. We hope our grandkids enjoy reading about our lives. It didn't take a lot back in the old days to have a good time.

Grandpa's Stories

THE GREAT DEPRESSION 1929-1942

I was born April 7, 1934 in Tulsa, Oklahoma to two great hard-working parents. With the help of some basic information from the internet, I'll put my family's life into context within America's darkest times since the Civil War. The Great Depression was the deepest and longest-lasting economic downturn in the history of the Western industrialized world. In the United States, the Great Depression began just after the stock market crash of October 1929 which sent Wall Street into a panic and wiped out millions of investors. It was eased a little when the USA supported England in WWII against Germany. And more when the Japanese attacked Pearl Harbor and we declared war against Japan in December 1941 and formally entered WWII. There were droves of men and women joining the Armed Forces. This put a lot of housewives to work filling all the jobs that had been always done by men.

The Melton Gang with Grampa Walt

OK, let us go back to 1929. Work was hard to find, food was not plentiful unless you had a pocket full of money, and crime was at an all-time high. People were stealing and robbing to survive. The US Government started a federal program called The Civilian Conservation Corps (CCC). CCC was a public work relief program that operated from 1933 to 1942 in the United States for unemployed, unmarried men from relief families as part of the New Deal.

1

Grandpa's Stories

My Uncles Chester and Efton were a part of this program. These two were brothers of my mother. They had very much to do with building our National Parks all over the country. This program should not be confused with the WPA that started up a little later.

The Works Progress Administration (renamed in 1939 as the Work Projects Administration; WPA) was the largest and most ambitious American New Deal agency, employing millions of unemployed people (mostly unskilled men) to carry out public works projects, including the construction of public buildings and roads. In a much smaller but more famous project, Federal Project Number One, the WPA employed musicians, artists, writers, actors and directors in large arts, drama, media, and literacy projects. Almost every community in the United States had a new park, bridge, or school constructed by the agency. A lot of our own Berryhill School (all of the native stone buildings) was built by the WPA.

The Laura Prince clan—see Note at the end of story

My mother and dad both belonged to very close-knitted families that always stuck together through thick and thin. My dad would take advantage of any opportunity to make a little money or work any job. In 1932 he was called upon to go to Fort Sill, Oklahoma for training to drive big trucks in the event we were to enter a war. This was long before we entered the war against Germany, so our Government knew something was brewing. These were mostly men who had been classified 4A during the draft. My dad was flat footed which excluded him from serving. This training qualified my dad to hire out driving about any kind of truck. I have an old letter that he wrote to my mother from Fort Sill when my sister was still a small baby. I was not yet born.

Grandpa's Stories

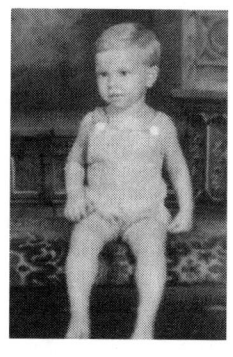

I don't remember this, but I was told by my mother, that we once lived on the property of Crystal City Amusement Park where my dad was the overseer of the park and also bouncer at Casa Loma, which was the dance hall where all the Big Bands came to play for dances. While we were living there Mom tells me one morning she answered a knock on the door and when she opened the door there was an Oklahoma Highway Patrolman holding me in his arms. He asked her if I belonged to anyone there. He said he saw me sitting in the middle of Highway 66 with my dad's ten-gallon hat and all he saw at first was the hat with two little legs sticking out. Needless to say he probably saved my life.

Once when I was about two my Uncle Efton was working in Dayton, Ohio. He wrote my dad a letter and told him that there was work there for him if we could get up there. We took off for Dayton: Dad, Mom, my sister, and I, along with Grandma Doshie and Walt. We would drive a while and stop and my dad would go try to find some kind of work to buy something to eat and some gasoline to get a little further down the road. I'm told it took us about two weeks to get there. We would camp along the highway. I think we probably camped near Uncle Efton until my dad was called back to Oklahoma to do the work he was trained for of driving trucks in WWII.

I also remember living in a tent city at Newblock Park along with hundreds of families. At this time, it was about the largest park in Tulsa. It was located on the north side of what is now Charles Page Blvd. along a red clay bluff. I remember our tent had a dirt floor but Mom would sweep it every day. I'm told that someone in the city would bring back a bacon rind or some meat bones and would make a pot of soup or beans and pass it on down to the next tent. Times were hard.

On top of all that the was the Dust Bowl, which was caused by plowing up all the deep rooted grasses. When the drought came in three waves,

Grandpa's Stories

1934, 1936, and 1939–40, the unanchored soil turned to dust which often reduced visibility to 3 feet or less. I'm guessing it was rough times.

When I was seven Dad bought our first house. It was on West Eighth St. in Tulsa. 5935 West 8th St. It had once been an old barn at Lake Station but was moved to this location and converted into a very nice two-story house. The only two-story on the block. A lot of the people there thought we were rich. Dad paid $ 1750.00 for it and the monthly payments were $17.25 a month. Most of the time my room was upstairs and bigger than most of the places I had ever lived. I say that because there were several times we had to make room for family members. When Uncle Chester got out of the Army after WWII he moved in with his new wife and step-daughter. Later Efton and his three children lived with us for a few months. Edward, when he came back for WWII, lived there for a while. After my sister Jeri married, Mom rented out her old room to a young lady.

I remember going into the back yard and there was a pile of coal. I asked Dad what that was. He told me, "Son, you know those stoves in the house?" I said yes. He said, "Well, when you see the coal bucket getting empty you come out here and fill it up and bring it back in. You will just pick up a clod like this and hit it with the hammer and break it up in to smaller pieces." I was elated. I said, "Daddy, do you mean I'll never have to chop kindling again?" He said, "That's right, Son."

My dad drove pop delivery trucks for several different soda pop bottling companies like Pepsi Cola, Seven Up, Dr. Pepper, and Royal Crown Cola that I know of. He was also an entrepreneur. Whenever he had the chance he would buy or take over some business that was having trouble or whatever. I remember him having a pool hall, upholstery company, mattress company, and a cafe. My mother ran the cafe and my dad would hire someone he knew and trusted to run the other businesses.

Remember I said he would do about anything that would pay off. One day my Uncle Efton came by and told us he had ditched a load of whiskey up in Colorado when the Colorado Highway Patrol got after him. He told my dad if he wanted to go up after it he would tell him where he hid it. This

Grandpa's Stories

was during the times of prohibition in Oklahoma. Dad got into his 1937 Lincoln Zephyr and went after it. (Besides the Zephyr, Daddy also had a big Indian (this was a popular brand) motorcycle that he would get on and take for rides.) The next day when my dad came back he had four cases of Four Roses Irish whiskey. He carried it right up our front steps. About an hour later a deputy sheriff knocked on our front door. Dad went to the door and saw who it was. He blocked the view because the whiskey was setting right there on the piano bench. He said, "Well, hello Oates," he knew the guy. "What do you need?" He told my dad he had a report that he was carrying liquor into the house and asked if he could come in? Dad said, "Do you have search warrant?" He said no and my dad told him to go get one and he would be welcome to come on in. He left, and when he came back in a couple of hours Dad had moved the liquor under the house where he kept his home brew.

Aunt Helen with my sister Jeri

Bob Thorpe

Aunt Helen, my Aunt Irene in Blackwell, Oklahoma told me, that my Aunt Helen was who kept everyone in the family eating during a lot of the depression. She was associated with some pretty shady characters. As a matter of fact, she was married to Bob Thorpe, first cousin to the great athlete Jim Thorpe. Bob was gunned down by the Tulsa Police during an attempted drug store robbery. My cousin Edward Melton was living with them at that time. He told me that their next door neighbors were Bonnie Parker and Clyde Barrows. He remembered it was on North Cincinnati St. I have several photos of Aunt Helen, Bob Thorpe, and some of her shady friends. She was a beautiful lady. I remember her very well. She is buried in our family plot at Memorial Park.

Grandpa's Stories

Dad

I remember the day we were called and told my dad was dead, February 14, 1942. He had been called up to do the war duty he had trained for at Fort Sill and he was driving an oil tanker southwest of Tulsa in Creek County and went into a diabetic coma and crashed. He wasn't killed instantly but got out of the wreckage and went to the nearest farmhouse. That was when Mom bought our family plot at Memorial Park.

About a year later Mom married my Uncle Iva Ross Saulmon and he became my stepfather. Pop was the half-brother of my dad and one of the finest men I ever knew. I was never treated like a stepson. My mother never had to work again. He was a good provider. At that time, he was a tool designer for Spartan Aeronautics working directly for J. Paul Getty. He designed the tool for making the camping trailer call the Spartan Manor. After the war he bought a shoe shop in Brookside at 35th and Peoria. I worked there for him a lot. Nuff said.

Pop with Mom

July 2016

Note—Grandma Laura Prince was the mother of both my dad and of Pop. She married M. D. Saulmon and had four sons, Charlie, Fred, Iva, and Bill. She left them to marry Lon Layton, the father of my dad, Thomas Alvin Layton. She also had Edgar and Edna with Lon. Lon, Edgar and Edna all died in the flu epidemic of 1918. Later Laura married Jim Mitchell; they had a son, Ray.

Grandpa's Stories

THE RATTLER

Thinking back to my earliest memories in life, a hot summer day at my grandparent's farm on Turkey Mountain comes to mind. Turkey Mountain is located in southern Tulsa County, Oklahoma between the Arkansas River on the east and Union road on the west and south, 51st South on the north, and 71st South on the south.

The old farm, when I look back on it, really wasn't much to shout about. It was an old worn out and abandoned oil field with old pipe and oil field junk everywhere you looked. There were a lot of areas where nothing would grow because of salt water spills.

Granma Doshie Belle and Grandpa Walt

The old farm house sat in the middle of one of these spots. There most likely wasn't more than five or six blades of grass on the acre where the house and barn sat. About forty or fifty feet from the front porch was an old rocking chair. One very hot summer day I was in the old rocker, rocking as hard as I possibly could, really having fun. All of a sudden I sensed something was wrong. I looked down to the ground and saw this humongous rattle snake which was striking at the front of the old rocker. It seemed to be very upset about something and was trying to get into rocker with me. I was old enough to know about snakes and immediately knew this was not a good situation to be in. I started screaming as loud as possible. All the doors and windows on the old farm house were open because of the heat, so I was easily heard by everyone within a quarter of a mile.

My grandma Doshie Belle and my mother came running out of the house, and my grandpa Walt came running from the barn. The first one to arrive on the scene was Grandpa's old German shepherd dog. His name was Dusty. He had come from under the old house which was probably the coolest place he could find. Dusty was running as fast as he could. I believe

7

Grandpa's Stories

he could sense the urgency in my screams. Without hesitation or even slowing down, Dusty grabbed that old rattler in his teeth and headed straight for the corn field with about two feet of rattle snake sticking out of each side of his mouth. Dusty was shaking the rattler as hard as he could.

Grandpa Walt grabbed me from the old rocking chair as he and Mom started looking for snake bites on me. Luckily the rattler hadn't bitten me. We could hear Dusty tearing that old rattler to pieces out there in the corn field. Dusty emerged from the corn field and came back to the front yard and laid down on the shady side of the water well. We knew that Dusty had been bitten several times. He wouldn't eat anything for several days, and would just lay around in the shade and look at you with his big brown eyes. A few days later Dusty was up and running again, acting like and knowing that he was the family hero.

2001

A SHORT STORY ON SHOES

I remember when I was still just a small kid growing up in Tulsa, Oklahoma. In the summertime almost every kid I knew went barefooted.

Usually about a week before school would start, Mom would take my sister and me to town to get a new pair of shoes to start school in. As I recall, there were two stores where we could buy shoes, Thom McAn, and Kinney. I remember Kinney had the x-ray thing that you stood on and it showed all the bones in your foot and what size shoes you needed.

There were two kinds of tennis shoes on the market at that time, Keds and PF Fliers. We had a big choice, you could get black or white, low tops or high tops. We would usually get a pair of boots of some kind for winter. Mine would be cowboy boots of which there were two kinds also--Acme and Justin. Sometimes I would get a pair of hunting boots with the little side pocket on the ankle for a pocket knife. Boy, that was neat!

Back in those days you wore a pair of shoes until they were either totally gone or you outgrew them. There were several shoe repair shops around town, usually one in the neighborhood you lived in that would put on half soles and new heels and dye the scuffs so when you got them back, it was like a new pair of shoes. I can remember all the boys and even some of the girls would completely wear out the toes of their shoes from playing marbles on the school ground. I remember my sister had a pair of what I called Drum Major boots she wore in the winter, always white. I know very little about girl's shoes, but I remember they wore high top white dress shoes with three straps around the ankles, and black patent leather shoes with a bow on the toe called Mary Janes. I remember high school girls wearing black and white saddle oxfords, and also the penny loafers.

When I was seventeen I bought my first pair of custom made cowboy boots. There was a saddle and boot shop by the name of Mock's at the Tulsa Stockyards, which at that time was located on the Sand Springs Line (now renamed Charles Page Blvd.) between Tulsa and Sand Springs. I hung around the stockyard quite a bit. I started cleaning out cattle trucks there when I was about eleven years old. I would get a fifty cents a truck and I could do three or four trucks in a day. It. sure beat mowing lawns for fifteen cents each and that took about four hours to do one. My dad told me one time, "There was no limit what a man could make shovelin' the <u>blank</u> out of the trucks, just like picken' cotton, sky was the limit." It took forty trucks to buy that pair of boots.

When I went in to the USAF we had to box up everything we brought with us but our toothbrush and razor. They gave us two pair of brogans and one pair of dress shoes of which none really fit very good. I think they only make about three sizes for the Military.

By the time my son was in school, there was a new tennis shoe all the basketball players were wearing called Converse. I wonder how many different kinds there are now?

July 2002

Grandpa's Stories

MY SCHOOL DAYS

It is not a vivid memory, but the first school I attended was Washington Irving Elementary (1938-39) located on Nogales Street between Archer and Admiral Streets. Irving had what was called a Pre-Primary class for four year olds. Once Mom made me stay home because the weather was so cold. It was said that I snuck out of the house and went to school, not bothering to put on a coat. My teacher wanted to know where my coat was. I told her that I didn't have one. The teachers chipped in some money and someone took me home to get my mother to take me to buy me a coat. Mom told them I had a coat. I got ran over by a Yellow Cab while going to school there. I must not have been hurt too bad! I can recall the name of one kid, Jimmy Larkin. Strange I would remember that. We lived in a duplex just off 3rd and Maybelle in Tulsa. Just out the back door were the railroad tracks that ran between Tulsa and Sand Springs. Just to the right from our back door you could see the 3rd Street Viaduct. I have been told that a bootlegger by the name of Martin Edwards lived in the other side of this duplex. Just around the corner on 3rd St. was the Pure White Dairy. (Not there anymore.) The place we lived on Maybelle was taken out when Interstate 244 was built across Tulsa.

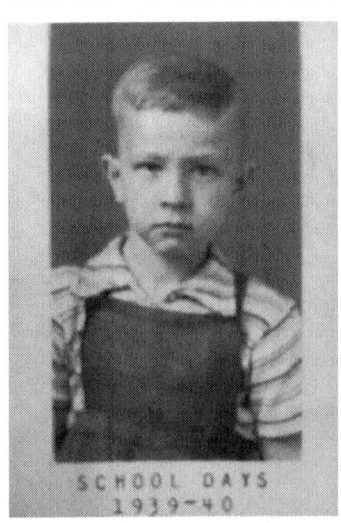
SCHOOL DAYS
1939-40

The next school was Lee Elementary located at 21st and Cincinnati. I must have been in Kindergarten. Next was Mark Twain Elementary on the Sand Springs Line which is now called Charles Page Blvd. I remember we lived in a little shotgun house on 4th Street about 3500 block West.

James Whitcomb Riley is the first school I really remember well. I started second grade there. Riley was located between Charles Page Blvd. and 8th Street at 57th West Ave. We lived at

Grandpa's Stories

5935 W. 8th St. in a big two-story house. I learned later that this house had been a barn which had been built further west at Lake Station and moved to this location. I remember my dad gave $1750.00 for it and our house payments were $17.25 a month. Mom and Dad had a little corner cafe on the corner of Charles Page and 60th W. Ave. just about 150 feet from our back gate. We were living here when World War II started.

I can remember all my teachers at Riley, even the principal, Mr. Hager. I guess the several spankings he gave me made a lasting impression. Mrs. Harper was our music teacher and everyone loved her. She would strive to make music fun for everyone. Mrs. Athens was over the library and she would read to us. I cannot recall anyone that could make a book come alive as she did. She would have everyone wanting to be there the next day to see what was going to happen in whatever book she was reading. The book I remember best was *Black Beauty*. Mrs. Langford was my 4th grade teacher. She was responsible for me having my tonsils and adenoids removed. She discovered that I was having trouble hearing the lessons; she told my mother and my tonsils were taken out. Mrs. Southern was one of my favorite teachers. I made many friendships from that little school and the neighborhood that have lasted all these many years.

From Riley I went to Roosevelt Jr. High School. This was really a new experience. This school was about four miles from our home just north and west of downtown Tulsa. We rode the streetcar to a stop at Archer and Elwood Streets. From there it was a thirteen block walk, uphill both ways (not really, it just seemed like it). At this point of my education kids came from several different grade schools so it was a lot like starting school all over again. You were in a class with a lot of strangers. I adapted quickly and made lots of friends from that school. I was on the football team there until they discontinued it my ninth grade year. I remember the principal Mr. Brown. He also made some lasting impressions on me. (grin) I could never forget Mrs. Culp who taught Social Studies. I was always getting into trouble in her class. She hated snakes and spiders. I could never forget the Roosevelt Jamboree my 8th grade year. This was a talent show that was held annually. Willis Houser and I did a skit with me playing guitar dressed as a girl and him a country hick playing a wash tub bass fiddle. We did a remake of Jo Stafford and Spike Jones' rendition of "Temptation." We got lots of laughs.

Then came Central High School at 6th and Cincinnati. This was really a big change. At that time there were only four high schools in Tulsa: Central, Rogers, Webster, and Booker T. Washington, which was all black at that time as this was prior to desegregation. There were about 3000 students at Central then. As I recall I had not one student in my homeroom that I knew. Midway through my junior year the Korean War broke out. There were several of us with the belief that we would lose this war if we didn't enlist.

I went through several short classes while in the USAF. The main being Aircraft & Engine School at Sheppard AFB in Wichita Falls, TX. I later attained my GED and when I got out of the USAF I enrolled in The Oklahoma School of Accounting where after five long hard years of night school I received an associate degree in Accounting. This was the first time in all my schooling that I received straight "As." I guess it was because for the first time in my life I was going to school because I wanted to.

HOBOS, TRAMPS, OR BUMS

First, let's try to define Hobos, Tramps, and Bums. Wikipedia says a hobo is a migratory worker who is willing to work for his keep. Tramps never work if it can be avoided, he just likes to travel. A bum is too lazy to work or travel except when he is propelled by the local law enforcement to move on. The hobo population really grew during the years of the Great

Depression. No work, no prospect, a lot of young men hit the road in search for employment. They could be frequently seen along railroads and major highways across the nation either hoping for a slow freight train or hitch hiking.

We lived just between both the Arkansas River and the Katy Railroad tracks. We would get them from both directions. I don't know how my mom could tell the difference but she could. At that time no one had air conditioning and always kept their windows open. If they were cooking or maybe baking a pie the aroma could be smelled for miles around, a natural drawing card for a hungry hobo. I remember them coming into the little cafe my mom ran on the corner of the Sand Springs Line (now renamed Charles Page Boulevard) and 60th West Avenue and asked Mom if she had any work to be done for something to eat. If he was a hobo she would tell him yes and then feed him, then assign him a job she wanted done. If he was in the cafe she would let him wash all the dirty dishes and sweep the floor with never a gripe from him. If he was a bum she would tell him to just keep moving on.

I can remember down on the Arkansas River near downtown Tulsa there was a huge Hobo Village. They would build them some type of little lean-to to keep the elements off and store their belongings while they were out looking for something to eat or work to earn some money. There was always a pot of stew on the fire waiting for anyone that showed up hungry. I've been told that there was a code of "Honor" at these camps that you never bother anyone or try to take something that did not belong you. Sounds to me like a great code.

THE OLD BOX

Last summer Beverly and I were cleaning the garage up a little. I was going through the old wooden box that I had kept junk, pipe fittings, etc. in for the last forty-some years and was going to make a repair to it. I would think that every household would have a catch-all of some kind for

Grandpa's Stories

leftover repair stuff like this box. One side had cracked about three inches down from the top and come loose. Beverly asked me what I was doing and I told her I was fixing this old box. She said, "That's a very interesting looking old box. Where did you get it?" I told her that it was a box that some of my dad's books had come in when I was a small boy. I told her that I could remember the set of books that had come in the box. They were big blue books that Dad kept in a lawyer's bookcase that set in the dining room. I can remember many times my dad would sit in his easy chair and read from these books; later I read them.

Beverly told me she wanted the box if I could fix it and clean it up a bit. She wanted to put it in the den where we have several old keepsakes. I proceeded to make the repair and clean some tar that had hardened in the bottom of the box. The old box cleaned up pretty well. It was a neat old box with finger joints. Pressed into two sides of the box was the black lettering "ADAMS 'MARCH of DEMOCRACY,' 5 volumes, Charles Scribner's Sons."

Beverly took the old box into the den and placed it on our fireplace hearth and set a picture of my family taken about 1937 or so on it. In the photo were my mom, dad, my sister and I. When I saw it I told Beverly it would be neat if we had the books that came in it, but they had been gone for a long time. Beverly called our daughter Melody, "the librarian," in Cleveland, Ohio and was telling her about the old box. After this conversation Melody decided to make an attempt at finding a set of these books which would now be considered antique and rare. Later Melody called and said to be on the lookout for some books she was having mailed to our house. In a couple of weeks, we found books on our front porch that had been delivered by UPS. I took them out of the box and found five big blue volumes of *The March of Democracy: A History of the United States*, by James Truslow Adams printed in New York by Charles Scribner's Sons in 1932. I'm in the process of reading these books again at the present time and finding them very interesting.

April 2005

HUNTING

Growing up in the 1940s everybody I knew hunted for wild game. While some hunted for sport, most hunted to put food on the table. All of my uncles and cousins hunted. Deer and wild turkey had nearly become extinct during the depression and were few and far between. Most hunting in Oklahoma was rabbit or squirrel.

The year I turned 12 my parents bought me a 22-caliber rifle. It was a single shot and the sweetest little gun on earth, I thought. As long as I could remember back, I had tagged along on family hunts but had never been allowed to shoot any of the real guns. I had my trusty Daisy "Red Rider" BB gun and could pop tin cans pretty easy with it, so adjusting to a 22 rifle was easy for me.

I remember very well that I could hardly wait for the following Sunday for Pop to take me squirrel hunting as they were in season. After squirrel season there would be no hunting until after the first snow of winter and that would be for rabbits. It was said that you should never eat a wild rabbit before first snow because you could get rabbit fever, which was bad. Pop had a single shot 12-gauge shotgun that he had bought it at an auction sale in 1925 for twenty-five cents. It didn't have a firing pin when he got it but he fashioned a new one from a ¼ inch bolt. I never saw Pop miss a running rabbit with that old gun. He shot a few quail on the fly when we would scare one up. I still have that old gun in my gun case. When I was in Jr. High School there was a classmate of mine that always wanted to go hunting with us. Her name was Carlita Owens; she loved tromping around in the woods with us and would always carry our game. Sometimes she would complain when she had to carry a gut shot rabbit, but that didn't happen often. I never saw Carlita after Jr. High.

Grandpa's Stories

A friend of mine, Van Martin, had a stepfather that had a large farm out west of Sand Springs near Shell Creek Lake. No one lived on the place but he used it to store large construction equipment that he used in his business. On several occasions about 4 or 5 of us would go out there on Friday or Saturday evening to hunt for bobcats. They were plentiful in that area. There was an old huge two-story farmhouse there. Upstairs there were four big windows facing the courtyard. We would bait the courtyard with chicken blood and it would always attract a bobcat sometime before daylight. We would keep records to make sure whose turn it was to get first shot at it. I think we all eventually got a bobcat. A few times a coyote or a wolf made an appearance, too bad for them.

A few years later while in the USAF, I was in Fairbanks, Alaska where big game was plentiful. You could see herds of caribou, some times as many as 3000 crossing the Alcan Highway. I never tried the caribou but I did get to shoot me a moose. We were flying a test hop and saw a huge bull moose over by Silver Lake not far from the base. After we landed, Carl Lord and I drove out there. I was shooting an old Remington Pump 30-06 with a Hexicon barrel. My shot was over a hundred yards; I thought I had missed but the moose, he ran about 100 feet, then went down. I had the opportunity to shoot a bear once but good judgment prevailed.

After I was married, my good friend Bill Sasser and I got involved in wolf hunting. Wolves were really hard to locate and track so Bill and I made a trap and would bait it with a live chicken. On one occasion, we were just getting ready to leave Bill's house to go bait the trap when Bill's wife Shirley called out that she had us a sandwich and a cup of coffee made. I was standing there holding the chicken and asked what was I going to do with this bird? My friend, Eddie Youngblood said, "No problem, get me a piece of string." Bill went into the house and came out with a ball of twine. Eddie cut off about 3 feet of the string and laid it out in a straight line on the porch. He then took the bird from me and set it down on the porch at the end of the string, putting one hand over the chickens head he slowly lowered its head and slowly moving his hand down over the eyes and beak, down along the string about 2 feet. Then Eddie turned around and said, "Let's eat." That dumb chicken just stood there gazing down the string totally hypnotized. Eddie said, "He will still be there when we get through eating." He was. When we came out from eating the chicken had not moved a muscle.

There was a farm out north of Prue where we hunted a few times. The farmer told us once that he saw a pack of wolves not long ago being led by a birddog. I thought the fellow was crazy. One day, Bill and I were laying out in his meadow trying to draw something using a turkey call. Bill was really good at making a turkey in distress call. After a couple of hours, we detected a movement back in the timber. Maybe 15 minutes later a very large birddog appeared right at the timberline. He was a German Short Hair Pointer, he stood there for at least another 15 minutes listening to Bill's turkey in distress, then disappeared back into the timber. We never saw him again.

A while later I got a birddog and started hunting for quail and occasionally did some duck hunting, mostly over decoys. I really loved hunting but eventually as retirement came along, it was no longer fun getting up at 4:00 a.m. and walking around all day on bad knees. Now I leave the hunting to the young.
2016

GRANDMA DOSHIE

Theodocia Belle "Doshie" Teeters, my grandmother, was born November 17, 1888 in Lockwood, Dade County, Missouri. She was the tenth of seventeen children. Her mother and father both were German. The Teeters family had migrated from Germany, Pennsylvania, Ohio, and Iowa, to Missouri and Oklahoma. After the Civil War her father and mother had left Ohio and journeyed west to Webster County, Iowa right in the heart of Sioux Indian country near Fort Dodge. Grandma Doshie's grandfather was a Methodist minister and set up the first church there in

Grandpa's Stories

Webster County in their log cabin. I'm told they always had a lamp in the window to guide any lost soul. My great-grandfather George Washington Teeters moved his family to Lockwood, Missouri just a few years before Doshie was born.

    I never had the opportunity to meet many of Grandma's siblings but the ones that I did were some of the best people I ever knew. I remember Rose, Alma, and Ethel, and that was about it. Rose lived here in Tulsa for a while, Ethel at Stroud, Oklahoma. You could never forget her. She had five names, Ethel Celestine Josephine Pearl Teeters. Alma lived on a big farm near Seminole, Oklahoma.

Grandpa Dave and Doshie Melton, l-r Chester, Helen, Efton, George

    Grandma first married a very tall thin man named David Edward Melton, 6 feet 4 inches. David was a Square Dance fiddler and caller. I'm told that Grandma Doshie could do a jig or reel as well as anybody. David Edward brought quite a bit of heritage into our family. His mother was Anna C. Goodnight and was also connected to the Chisholm line. Both were famous pioneer families with cattle trails named after them. David Edward's father was Thomas Jefferson Melton. This man was at one time a soldier under General Custer in the 7th Cavalry. He was discharged just before the big massacre.

Grandpa's Stories

Sometime after 1922 my grandma married Walter H. Holmes who had just been released from the Army and told to go home and die. He had too much shrapnel in the body from WWI that was inoperable. He fooled a lot of people on how long he did live. I remember Grampa Walt very well and feel I'm a better person for knowing him. He had a lot of character.

Grandma was a praying woman. She always would say a prayer for anyone who asked her to. If you were sitting at her table, you never took a bite until she had prayed for everyone at the table by name.

Grandpa Walt and Grandma Doshie Holmes

If my grandma ever cooked on anything but a wood burning stove, I never knew about it. If there was ever a better cook than her, I never heard about that either. It was always a delight to sit at her table. Grandma didn't know of most of the spices that are used today but always managed. She also never opened many tin cans in her lifetime. Many a glass fruit jar because she canned almost everything they ate or picked it fresh from the garden. I remember she had hundreds of those green fruit jars that had a wire bail to hold the lid on tight. If there was meat on the table, it was something her and Walt had raised or Walt had caught or shot. I remember watching Grandma wring the necks of chickens two at a time with one in each hand.

Her cookies and pies, if you have never ate pies cooked in a wood burning oven you have missed out on life! When my grandparents made a trip to a grocery store their purchases would be for salt, pepper, sugar, cinnamon, flour, baking soda. I'm talking strictly staple items that they did not grow themselves.

Grandpa's Stories

Grandma Doshie and Grandpa Walt

I remember Grandma cooking and canning fish that Walt had caught that would beat any kind of canned fish on the market today. And when she really put on a breakfast for the family it would usually include biscuits, fresh eggs right out of the hen house, gravy and potatoes, and probably some of the fresh home pork sausage that Walt had just made or some of the ham he had smoked. This kind of food would make some people want to throw rocks at some of these people now on television who cook with millions of folks watching and making millions of dollars. Chicken and dumplins, now you talk about mouthwatering. And you should taste some of the jellies and jams she would put up. Well, I just have to stop talking about her food. You could gain weight just talking about it.

I remember going out into the field to help pick something and taking it to the local store and trading it for something else. You could always take fresh eggs there and swap for anything. So I'm guessing there must not have been all the restrictions placed on grocery stores at that time.

Grandma passed away in September 1967 so I was blessed to know her for about 33 years. She was always a joy to be around. I never really saw her mad at anyone or heard her say a derogatory word of anyone. She would have to be classified as a rare specimen in today's world. They just don't make many like that anymore.

Grandma got dementia just before she died. She would ask my mom what in the world was she talking about. Mom would tell me that it was about something that had happened many years ago. Gosh, from writing this little article I realize I still miss my Grandma. God bless you, Grandma.

2016

Grandpa's Stories

GRAMPA WALT

Grampa Walt at right and his Brothers

My Grampa Walt was a pretty colorful fellow. When I was a kid he would tell me stories about when he was young. One story I remember well was about when he and his brothers first came to Tulsa. They had come north from Texas on horseback and had been on the trail for several weeks. As they rode into Sapulpa, Oklahoma they were going to have their first good hot meal since leaving Texas. That had been their main topic of conversation all day long. At that time Sapulpa was a bigger town than Tulsa. They rode into town just before sunset. As they were tying their horses to the hitching post in front of the Chinaman's Restaurant, the Chinaman came to the door and turned his open sign around to the closed position. Grampa Walt and his brothers had their mind set on some good hot food and started pounding on the door. The Chinaman came to the door to explain to them that he was "velly solly" but he was closed for the day. Not to be denied a good hot meal they put the Chinaman in a cotton sack and hung it in the back room while they warmed up some leftovers to eat. After they had eaten, they left some money on the counter and hightailed it for Tulsa, leaving the poor old Chinaman yelling and kicking in the back room hanging in the cotton sack.

On one occasion I saw Grampa shoot a man. We were sitting on the front porch of the old farm house in Salina, Oklahoma. There was Grampa Walt, my dad, two of my uncles, Chester and Efton, my cousin Edward, and me. The old Indian who lived on the property east of Grampa's farm rode up to the gate, opened it, and rode on through leaving the gate open behind him. He always came home that way because it was a shortcut to

21

Grandpa's Stories

his house. Grampa called out to him to go back and shut the gate so the stock wouldn't get out. The old Indian was drunker than a skunk. He yelled back to Grampa, "Go to hell, you old S.O.B." Before anyone knew what was about to happen, Grampa jumped up, reached inside the front door, got his shotgun, and blowed the Indian right off that horse. My dad and Uncle Chester picked the Indian up off the ground and took him to the hospital at Pryor, Oklahoma. A couple of hours later a Deputy Sheriff drove up to the gate, got out, and started to open the gate. Grampa, reaching for his shotgun again, shouted out to the Deputy, "I wouldn't open that gate if I was you. This is private property." The Deputy hollered back, "Now Walt, you know darn good and well that I have to ask you some questions and write up a report on what just happened here. Good night, Walt, you could have killed him, you know." Walt told the Deputy to go ahead and ask all the questions he needed to, saying "I can hear you just fine from there." The Deputy did stay at the gate and wrote his report. I guess that was the end of that, because the Indian didn't file any charges against Grampa. He got out of the hospital about three or four days later. He never cut across Grampa's property any more.

A while later I was glad Grampa hadn't killed the old guy. I was out one evening looking for one of the cows and got lost back in the hills. I was walking around in the darkness yelling, hoping someone would hear me and come to my rescue. All of a sudden I felt someone grab my arm. I looked up and could barely make out that it was the old Indian who Grampa had shot. He said, "Aren't you Walt's grandson?" I said, "Yes sir, I am." I was scared to death. He said, "Come on, I'll show you the way home." He led me through the woods to the bottom of the hill where the cistern was. I could see the lamps burning at the house. The old Indian stopped and said, "You can make it from here. This is as close as I go." I was really relieved and thanked him for showing me the way home.

Another time I remember well was when me and Grampa Walt went to the little cafe in Salina where my cousin Bonny was working as a waitress. My grandma and grampa were Bonny's legal guardians. We were sitting there waiting for the cafe to close when two soldiers started trying to make out with her and take her home. Bonny was only thirteen at that time but was very well developed. I was just 15 at the time. Walt looked over at me and said, "No matter what happens here I don't want you to get involved, do you understand that?" I said yes. Grampa got up and went over and told the two young men to quit pestering Bonny. One of them kind of pushed Grampa and said, "Go sit down and mind your own business, you old S.O.B." He hadn't got the last syllable out when Grampa came up with a right "haymaker" that lifted the G.I. plum off the floor and he went crashing, knocking over a table and a couple of chairs. He turned around to the other one who was coming at him hard and fast. The young G.I. was swinging hard at Grampa's head but Grampa just ducked and drove his head right into his belly and drove him into the counter. The young G.I. tried to push Grampa away but Walt just kept pounding at his head. In seemed like a long time but actually only lasted a few seconds. When Walt backed away the young G.I. just kind of casually slid down to the floor. The cook and owner of the cafe by that time was out there wondering what all ruckus was about and said "Walt, do you need any help? I guess not." At that time Walt was about 57 years old but looked like 80 by today's standards.

Another memory of Grampa Walt is from November of 1952. I was home on leave for Thanksgiving. The whole family converged at Salina, Oklahoma at Grandma Doshie and Walt's little house. They had moved from the farm to town. There was a carnival going on at the armory there in Salina and I got cousin Clyde and we moseyed over to check it out. Me and Clyde rode the Ferris wheel then we came upon a game booth where you could win "Big Money." The guy called me over and said being as I was in uniform I could have the first play free. I was young enough to be suckered in. This game you turned over a bunch of ping pong balls and they rolled down a chute and fell in different numbered holes. He added the numbers and looked a chart to see just how many points I had earned for that roll. It took ten points to win one hundred dollars. That first roll I acquired five

Grandpa's Stories

points. Wow, I was already half way there. The cost of each roll was fifty cents. I gave the $.50 and rolled again; I wasn't very lucky that time. He added up the numbers and looked at the chart. No points, but it said that meant the price of rolling doubled. I gave him a one dollar bill and rolled once again. He added the numbers and eyed the chart. I had gotten ½ of a point. Next roll I got to add again making it cost $2.00 for each roll. Clyde said, "Connie, you're just going to lose your money."

    I got to noticing that I wasn't able to add the numbers before the operator turned them back for another roll. I soon got to where I was paying $8.00 a roll and was only up to 6 ½ points. On my next roll I grabbed the guy's arm before he could turn the ping pong balls back. He yanked away from my grasp and yelled, "What are you doing?" I said, "You've been cheating me and I want my money back." He said I was a bad sport and that I was through there. I looked around and I saw a couple of the other carnies coming over there. I said, "Come on Clyde, we're going home." I could smell trouble brewing if we stayed there and I didn't want to get Clyde hurt. He was only about fourteen at that time. When we walked into the house Grampa Walt looked at me and asked what's wrong. I said nothing. He jumped up and said, "Don't tell me that. I know when something ain't right." Clyde blurted out, "Connie got chiseled out of a bunch of money at the carnival." Walt asked how and I told him. He headed for the door and said, "Come on, boys, we're going over and get his money back." Walt led the way with my stepdad, Uncle Chester, Uncle Efton, and cousins Edward and Clyde. When we got to the armory grounds and started toward the game where I had lost the money, the Deputy Sheriff started over to us. He said, "What are you doing, Walt?" Walt looked at him and said, "You need to stand back. We're doing some family business." He got a funny look, and started back the other way.

Grandpa's Stories

Cousin Edward, Uncles Efton and Chester with Bonnie, Grandma Doshie and Mom

At that point Uncle Chester took the lead. When we all walked up the game counter, the guy that was cheating me stuck out his barrel chest and leaned out over the counter like he was daring anyone to advance. He had on bib overalls with no shirt and the black hair was literally boiling out above his bib. Uncle Chester reached over the counter and grabbed a handful of hair and started pulling him over the counter. I looked around to see if any of the other carnies were going to head that way. None of seemed to want anything to do with our group. The game carnie started screaming for Chester to let him down. His feet were completely off the ground. Walt said, "You cheated my grandson out of $47 and we want it now." He said, "Let me go and I'll give it to you, damm it. I can't reach it now." Efton reached over and moved his money till within reach and said, "You can now." The guy reached in and counted out $47. Chester said, "Hand it to my nephew. I stepped up and took the money out of his hand. Chester let go and said to the guy, "Have you had enough?" The guy just stood there and glared at us. Grampa Walt said, "Come on, boys, we're going home." We started walking back home and there stood that Deputy Sheriff. He asked Walt, "Well, did you get what you came after?" Walt didn't even answer him. When we got back to the house, he looked at me and said, "Son, I hoped you learned something today." We had a great Thanksgiving dinner and everyone had a wonderful day.

Grampa Walt had been wounded in France in WWI and was discharged from the Walter Reed Military Hospital near Washington DC in 1922. They told him to go home for he had six months or less to live. His body had so much shrapnel that it was impossible to remove it all without killing him. We buried him forty-two years later at Memorial Park on January 15, 1964. I guess you could say that Grampa Walt was pretty coarse and gritty I suppose, but I think that was the kind of true grit that helped to settle our country and held it for all these years. He wasn't a big man, but he sure acted like it once in a while.

WESTERN UNION

When I was 15, I worked for Western Union for a summer. The pay wasn't anything to brag about (35 cents an hour) but the job had lots of great fringe benefits, like 30 minutes off for lunch, getting to meet new people, lots of fresh air, lots of sunshine, lots of rain, etc. I rode a bicycle delivering telegrams.

The year was 1949 and the "City of Tulsa" was still the "Oil Capital of the World." At that time in history, it was said that 75% of all oil field equipment and oil field supplies used in the entire world were manufactured between Main Street in Tulsa and Main Street in Sand Springs. Tulsa was where all the action was. If you wanted to see a movie, go to the doctor, dentist, or lawyer you had to come to town. If you wanted to shop for clothing, you came to town. If you wanted to buy a car, you came to Tulsa. If you wanted a tool or car part, you came to town. That is where everything was, no malls, no shopping centers as we know them today. The Tulsa City Limits ended at Yale Ave. The only business establishments in a neighborhood would be a Mom & Pop grocery, drug store, or maybe a dry cleaning shop or cafe.

Those were the days when people dressed up to go to town. All the women would put on their best clothes and always a hat, most men also wore a hat. The hotels in Tulsa were always full and lots of deals going on. The streets of downtown Tulsa were always very busy and bustling not to mention that they were safe for anyone to be on.

Grandpa's Stories

Lunch: The Western Union was located in the southeast corner of the Mayo Hotel next to the alley between Boulder and Cheyenne on 5th Street. At lunch time I could go out the alley door, run north less than a block to 4th Street and right there next to the alley was Coney Island. This was Tulsa's original Coney Island ran by "Nick the Greek." I could order 2 full size Coney's, a sack of Fritos and a 12 oz. bottle of Pepsi Cola, pay with a quarter and get back 3 pennies. The old place sold a few years ago and moved across the street and west a half a block. It costs a little more now to eat there.

The highlight of my career at Western Union was when the premier of the movie "Tulsa" with Robert Preston, Susan Hayward, and Chill Wills was taking place in Tulsa. I was working that day and my boss handed me a telegram and told me to get over to the Hotel Tulsa and deliver the telegram to Robert Preston. I remember going to the room number given me. Each room had a solid door with louvered bat wing doors in front of them. The door was wide open and I could hear people talking through the louvered doors. I knocked on the door, Robert Preston said "Come on in, the door's open." All three of the stars were there: Robert Preston, Susan Hayward, and Chill Wills. Susan Hayward was about the prettiest woman I had ever seen in person. I don't really remember, but I was probably standing there with my mouth wide open. I handed the telegram to Mr. Preston, stood there for a moment as he started to read the telegram. As I started to turn around and leave, Chill Wills said, "Wait a minute boy, here you are." I stopped and he flipped me a half dollar. I thanked him and went on out. That was the biggest tip I remember getting.

There were a couple of guys with motor cycles and a few with automobiles that made the distant deliveries. Once my boss handed me a telegram and said, "Take this to Dawson." Dawson was a small community way out in the country between Pine and Apache on Yale Street. There was a lot of open country between Tulsa and Dawson at that time and it was a pretty good ride on a bicycle. The weather was good though, and it wasn't too bad. Another time he asked me to go to Broken Arrow in the rain and I told him no way. About that time one of the distant drivers came in and he gave it to him. At that time, Broken Arrow would have been at least a 3 hour trip each way.

Once I had a Singing Telegram to deliver. After I finished singing a guy in the room gave me a quarter and told me to forget about Broadway. Oh, those were the good old days.

January 2004

MY FIRST AUTOMOBILES

EVERY young man's dream is to turn sixteen and get his driver's license. I was lucky enough that my birthday fell on a weekday and just as soon as I got home from school I was able to go take the test. I was also lucky enough that I passed the test. My dad had let me drive the family car when we were out in the country from the time I was thirteen so I could handle the car pretty good. Grandma and Grampa Walt lived in Salina, Oklahoma and every weekend we went there to visit. There was never any traffic after we left Pryor, Oklahoma, so Pop would pull over and let me drive the rest of the way.

Very soon after I turned sixteen I purchased my first car. It was a 1929 Ford Model A Roadster with a ragtop and rumble seat. The cost was $35. I had saved my money for a long time to buy this little car. It would go about 58 miles an hour when you pushed the pedal to the metal. That was floor boarded. This car got me into a lot of trouble. Just about the time I got my car, the City of Tulsa installed two one-way streets. Boston Avenue was the northbound and Boulder was the southbound street. I was downtown and turned the corner at 3rd and Boston going the wrong way (south). A police car that was right behind me pulled me over. He very nicely told me I was going the wrong way on a one-way street and escorted me up and around the corner so I wouldn't have an accident. He was so nice and just warned me not to do that again.

Grandpa's Stories

About 30 minutes later I was going East on 11th St. when the light changed and the police car in front of me stopped so quick that I ran into the back of him. He stopped so quickly that as the rear of his car came up and the front of mine went down we locked bumpers. It took about six men to get us loose. You would never guess who the policeman was, right? The very one that had just been so nice to me. He asked, "You have just started driving, right?" I said yes, that I'd had my driver's license about a week. He told me about my car having mechanical brakes and newer cars having hydraulic brakes and told me to be careful. No ticket; he was a great guy.

My dream car used a lot of oil, mostly leaks, so I carried a five-gallon can of used oil in the back. One Friday night while Charlie Garroutte and I were cruising in Sand Springs, I turned a corner right by the Harmony Theater and the lug nuts on one of my wheels tore out leaving us with a three-wheeled car. We managed to get it into a parking place and phoned Mary's Cafe at Lake Station, just a mile or so up the road. Mary's husband had a car lot there in Sand Springs and I knew that he had a Model A on his lot. After I told him what had happened, he told us to go to his lot and take the spare tire off his Model A and use it. We could settle up with him the next day.

Lo and behold, Charlie was holding the flashlight and I was taking the spare tire off when the Sand Springs Police shined their spotlight on us. While they were booking us into jail I told them that we had permission to use that spare tire, to call Mary's Cafe and ask her husband. It didn't do any good. They put us in jail anyway without letting either of us make a phone call. Pretty soon they came back and brought us back into the office and started asking questions. They wanted to know where we had been stealing gasoline. When I said we hadn't stolen anything, they referred to the can in the back of my car. I told them it was used oil, but they didn't believe that either. One of the police kept pulling his leather gloves tighter like he was getting ready to hit me. I told him he was a sorry s.o.b. and that if he did hit me he was going to be in a lot of trouble. Anyway he didn't ever hit me. They took us back into the lockup.

Grandpa's Stories

The next morning, we were sitting there when Charlie's uncle, who was named Jack Garroutte (he was the Chief-of-Police), came walking through the jail. He stopped at the door of our cell, looked in and said, "Charlie, is that you? What are you doing in there?" Charlie told him what had happened and he wanted to know if we were hungry. We told him we were starving. He let us out and wanted to know if our parents knew where we were. Charlie told him that we were not allowed to phone anyone. He said first we were going to call our parents, then he was going to take us to a little cafe around the corner and feed us breakfast. After we were finished with breakfast we went over to the car lot where all this started and Mary's husband verified that I had called and had gotten permission to get the spare tire. At this time, we took the spare tire off, and Uncle Jack took us back to where we had left my car. Charlie and I put it on my car and we went home. I learned later that the policeman that had arrested us was fired from the Sand Springs Police Department.

My second car was a 1936 Ford Sedan. It ran like a Singer sewing machine. Going down the road you could not hear it running. While over in Prattville one day, I drove back on an old oil lease and hit a tree stump that was just tall enough to catch the bottom of my muffler. It folded it back like an accordion. On the way home a highway patrolman stopped me for making so much noise. When I told him what had just happened to my muffler he told me he believed me because he had seen me earlier that day and had not heard the noise. He told me to go home and put a new muffler on my car and he would forget about it. That car never left my back yard until I had saved enough money to buy a new muffler.

My next car was a 1939 Ford Deluxe. Sounds like I had a thing for Fords, doesn't it? My 1939 Ford Deluxe was a black two-door sedan. It looked good and ran good. I loved the sound of those old flat head V-8s. At the same time I owned this car, Uncle Efton had a 1937 Ford Sedan that would outrun about anything in Oklahoma. It was really souped up. I told Uncle Efton that if he ever decided to get rid of or trade it to give me first chance at it. Uncle Efton was my mother's brother, just a little older than she was.

Grandpa's Stories

He used this car to transport certain goods once in a while during the days of prohibition. One day he called me from Spavinaw, Oklahoma, where he ran a local bait shop. Efton said "Connie," which is what everyone called me back then, "if you still want the '37 you can have it for nothing. It is at your Grandma's house in Salina. If you come to get it, you need to bring the battery and wheels off your car. The highway patrol was after me and I rolled it over 8 times. I think you can get to Tulsa if you take your time."

The very next Sunday Pop and I took my battery and all four wheels from my car and headed for Salina. The old '37 was a real mess. It had no hood, trunk lid, or door on the driver's side. All the tires were blown out and the battery was torn out leaving one of the posts still in the battery cable. Efton had forgot to tell me that the radiator was all busted up and all the hoses for it and both motor mounts broken. Grampa Walt had some old 19 inch inner tubes that we made radiator hoses out of, as there were no auto parts stores open on Sunday. The radiator was leaking like a sieve. Grampa said we could plug up some of the leaks with a couple of cans of Prince Albert and a jar of mustard. It sounds crazy, right? But it did help a little. We also found two old 5-gallon cans to put extra water in, hoping it would get us to Pryor for a refill. We did manage to get to Pryor where we found a service station that had some real radiator stop leak. I bought about five cans of it and put it all in the radiator. Between Pryor and Claremore, a highway patrolman stopped me. He was about to write me a ticket for driving a wreck like that on the highway. When Pop pulled up and explained that we were trying to get it to Tulsa before it got dark, he told me to be very careful and to get it off the roads before dark. I got stopped one more time after we were in Tulsa, but he let it go so I could make it home before dark. I pulled the engine from the wreck and replaced the motor mounts and installed it in my '39. When we were finished with my car, it purred like a kitten, hummed like a Singer sewing machine, and ran like a stripped ape. This was just a few of the terms used in those days. The little '39 was so hot it would lay scratch in all three gears.

Grandpa's Stories

One afternoon while we were at Mary's Cafe several guys were looking it over when this character says, "Don't look like anything special to me." I asked, "What are you driving?" He pointed to his '36 Chevy Coupe. When I saw his old Chevy I kinda snickered, and tried really hard not to bust out with uncontrollable laughter. I told him it would leave his car standing. He said "Well sure, but you've got two more cylinders than my Chevy." I said "Yes, but you could take any two sparkplug wires off this Ford and put them in your glove compartment and it would still outrun your Chevy." He said, "You've got a bet." We each went into Mary's and gave her $10 to hold for the first one to come back in there. When we got back outside I opened the hood and told him to take any two sparkplug wires that he wanted to. He took the two front wires from the left side. My first thought was "Uh oh." I didn't even know if my car would even start or not like that. I cranked it up though and it was coughing and sputtering, but running. About that time I was thinking that my big mouth had just cost me $10. At that time what is now Charles Page Boulevard was Highway 51 and 64. As you came into Sand Springs there was a triangle and the road forked. On one side of the highway there was the Sand Springs Green House and Commander Mills on the other. We were to race to the Green House around the triangle and the first one back into Mary's was to pick up the money. Back in those days there was very little traffic on that road except early morning and the evening when everyone was going to and from work. We lined up side by side, revving up our motors. When giving the signal we both took off with this other guy leaving me there in a cloud of smoke. When we had gone about a mile, he was still about a 100 yards ahead of me but I was starting to close the gap. When I reached the triangle, he was about a quarter mile behind me. When I pulled into Mary's, I jumped out and ran into the cafe and told Mary to pour me a cup of coffee real quick. When he came in the door, I was taking a drink of coffee and was holding the $20 that we had given Mary when I looked up at him. He was a good sport about losing and handed me back my sparkplug wires.

Grandpa's Stories

Another time one of my best friends, Bobby Hall, had moved across town out near the Traffic Circle which was fairly new in those days. This was the intersection of Rt 66 and Rt 75, where there had been a number of head-on collisions. Traffic circles were being installed where two major routes intersected to cut down on these types of collisions. Yale was the city limits so this was out in the country. Bobby's dad, Cotton Hall, had just bought a new 1950 Mercury. It was a beautiful thing to behold. We were talking about how fast my '39 was when Cotton said we didn't know what fast was. He said my 39 wouldn't hold a candle to his Mercury. Bobby said, "Dad, don't bet on that or you might lose your money." He told him my car was really souped up. Cotton said "Well, just for fun let's go over on Pine and find out how fast it really is." At that time Mingo was Highway 75 and Pine was a gravel road all the way from Mingo to Yale Street. We lined up there at Mingo, and when Bobby gave us the go sign, we both let the hammer down on our cars. There was so much dust that I couldn't even see Cotton for about a half mile. In simple terms, my old '39 Ford ate Cotton's new Mercury's lunch. When we got back to Bobby's house, Cotton just said, "Well I'll be dammed. That car will run." A few months later I blew out that engine. I took the block to Sun Motor in Tulsa and had them vet and check the blocks for cracks to see if it could be rebuilt. When they were through they called me and recommended it be scrapped. It had so much work done on it. They said someone had done a great job of relieving the intake and exhaust ports and had bored the cylinders to .110 oversized and they were so thin it would be impossible to give any kind of guarantee on it. I was glad then that I still had my old motor to put back in.

A SHORT STORY ABOUT GEORGE

George Washington Rogers was a first cousin of my wife Beverly. I first met George after I began going out with Beverly. I later really got to know George very well from going to school with him and taking him fishing and rabbit hunting.

Grandpa's Stories

Beverly's Cousin George Rogers

To begin with, George was captured by the North Koreans during the Korean Conflict. He spent 31 months in what is now considered the "Valleys of Death." I have read books about them that indicate that less than 10 percent of the captives survived the "Valleys of Death." Therefore, very well named. I also served in the Korean War as a flight crew member on B-29s. George was captured in 1953 and released in in 1955. He was the first Tulsa POW released and sent back to Tulsa. I'm told that when the news that George had been released a local radio station here in Tulsa asked the people of Tulsa to donate money for a brand new automobile to present to George when he got home to Tulsa. His coming home present turned out to be a new 1955 Ford Deluxe. I remember George was still driving it when I first met him. George told me that when he was released his weight was 107 pounds. That was down from 205. He was in an Army hospital for about six months before he was able to return home. Beverly says they had opened his stomach up from top to bottom trying to fix his problems. When I first met George he had very little strength and would tire out easily.

After Beverly and I were married I started back to school to get a degree in accounting at the Oklahoma School of Accounting. George was also attending the school. We were in several classes together for about a period of two years. During those two years George asked me once to take him rabbit hunting. So he came over one Saturday morning and we went to the Sand Springs River Bridge and started down the railroad tracks headed west. George could not go down into the brambles and weeds to run the rabbits out of their cover so I did that part. George would walk along the tracks for an easier walk. It wasn't long until a cottontail ran up and over the tracks. I was allowing George to take the first shots. I mean to tell you that George popped that dude. We walked about ½ mile down the tracks and had four rabbits. I asked George how he was doing and he said I'm ready to turn around and go back. We got one more just before we reached the truck and came home. Over that winter I took George hunting six or seven times.

One night at class we had this nut that was always ranting and raving about "being better red than dead." He was what was called a "card carrying Communist," always promoting Communism. One evening while we were on recess he spouted off about being better off red that dead. George jumped up and grabbed him by the throat. George obviously knew how to kill a man quickly. I saw this immediately because I had received the same training in an Army Ranger Survival Training Course while in the USAF. George had his big hands wrapped this guy's neck and had both thumbs on his Adams Apple. I mean to tell you his eyes were bugged out. He was totally helpless. I jumped up and being at least ten times stronger than George I forced his hands loose from this idiot. When I was looking into George's eyes I saw a look I had never seen before, it even scared me. George had come completely unglued. This guy took off getting away from George and gasping for air. I knew that Dumbo would eventually get his air back, but I was concerned for George. I got him settled down and sat him down on a bench and got him a Coke from the machine. I just started talking calmly to George and he turned to me and thanked me and said let's get back to class. Shortly after I saw Dumbo and I told him, if I were you I would never talk about Communism any more around George. You're lucky to still be alive. If George hadn't been so weak your larynx and everything in your throat would have been completely crushed before I could have helped you. He said your friend is crazy. I said, "No, he knows what Communism is all about. He spent 31 months in red prison camps all over North Korea. If he hadn't been so weak you would already be dead. I'm not going to help you next time." From that point on when we came out for recess he would go the opposite way that we went. I never heard the word "Communism" out of his mouth again.

On some of our hunting or fishing trips I sometimes asked George about Korea. He would just look at me and tell me let's not talk about it. He told me once that all he was trying to do was to shake some of the memories. I never mentioned it again.

George graduated before I did and immediately went to work for the State of Oklahoma State Auditor in Oklahoma City. He later got a great offer from a CPA firm in Los Angeles. After I graduated George would call me and ask if I had tested out for my CPA yet and I would tell him that I had decided not to pursue accounting. George and I had both been in the same CPA preparation class together. He would tell me get to Oklahoma City and take the test that they had my Jaguar waiting out there with my name on it. I told him that I had no intention of moving my family to LA. He soon quit bugging me about coming out there. After he retired George moved back here and he started a horse ranch.

One incident I remember, I knew this guy at work at American Airlines that was into horses along with his son. I had heard that they were both a rough lot. The two of them had made a horse deal with George's next door neighbor that somehow went sour. The two of them came out and were beating the crap out of him in his front yard when George heard the commotion. George came running out with his shotgun as they were driving off. Lucky for them. The neighbor filed a law suit. The guy from American Airlines had seen George witness the beating, so he came to talk to George. George saw him pulling up in front of his house and met him with his shotgun in hand. Needless to say the guy didn't open George's gate to come in. This guy came to me at work and told me he heard I had a cousin over in Collinsville. I told him that my wife's cousin lived over there. He told me about this incident and I told him he was messing around with the wrong guy with George. "You're lucky he didn't blow your head off."

We saw George several times before he died at age 68.

Beverly had another first cousin, John Edward Rogers who was also a first cousin of George's that I considered a hero as well. John, or Eddie as we all called him, was at Pearl Harbor when the Japanese launched their brutal attack on the US. Eddie was a survivor of that battle. We have a DVD of his burial at sea. It was quite a ceremony.

Grandpa's Stories

MY GUITARS

 I don't remember how old I was when I got my first guitar. I earned it selling Rose Salve door to door. You could earn so many points from each little can of Rose Salve and in their catalog it would show how many points each item cost to get. I'm thinking it took me at least a year to get the guitar. It was a Stella guitar. You can Google Stella guitar and read the history that goes way back to the late 1800s. I didn't have the points to get the carrying case so it came to me in a cardboard box. It had a pick and a booklet to show you how to play it. My cousin Edward Melton who was nine years older than me had played stringed musical instruments for as long as I could remember. He was really talented. I don't remember this but Eddie would always tell me, "Connie, don't you remember when we would sit for hours and watch and listen to Grandpa Melton play his fiddle?" Grandpa was a square dance caller and fiddler and was pretty salty. Of course he had been doing this for 50 years.

 I tried to play Eddie's guitar a few times but I was left-handed and it was rather awkward. Back in that day there was no such thing as a left-handed guitar. I just simply took off the strings and turned them around and made my own left-handed guitar. Edward wouldn't allow me to mess with his. I don't blame him though. After I got my Stella I would sometimes play with Eddie when we were together.

 When I was in eighth grade at Roosevelt Jr. High we had a school annual program called the "Jamboree." A close friend, Willy Houser, and I decided to enter and perform our rendition of Jo Stafford's hit song Temptation. She did this with the Spike Jones Band. Willy Houser made a one string bass out of a 2x4 and a #2 wash tub and I played my guitar. These one string basses were called a washtub bass and go back a long way. You changed the tune of the one string by putting more or less stress on the string. Willy was pretty good at it. We were dressed up like hillbillies. Needless to say we were the hit of the whole entire show.

 There were a couple of friends who played that I got together with many times. I also played trumpet in school. After I went into the Air Force,

Grandpa's Stories

I have no idea what happened to my guitar. Mom didn't either. I didn't have my guitar in Alaska. But there was bar I went to a few times where a couple of Eskimos played and sung. One of them was a lefty and had his guitar strung up backwards. I noticed this immediately. I told him I played that same way and they wanted me to play and sing something for them. I remember I sung "There Stands the Glass" by Webb Pierce. This was a #1 song when I entered the Air Force. If you have never heard it, try Googling it. Every time I went in to this place they wanted me to do a couple of songs. When I got home from Air Force four years later, I went to Sears and bought a Harmony guitar. It was a blond color and rather pretty. I also bought a pickup to install on it and bought an amplifier. I could make a lot of noise with this rig. It didn't take long to find out I had kinda rusted up a little from the long layoff of playing.

After getting married I decided to take guitar lesson from Dick Gordon over in the Brookside area. He very quickly discovered that I was a lefty and was ready for the challenge. After getting my calluses hardened up again I was learning chords I never knew existed before. Dick Gordon was a notable guitar teacher here in Tulsa. He also taught my son Tommy guitar and later Beverly took ukulele lessons from him.

Later Beverly, my sister Jeri, and I formed a trio and started singing at church and sometimes at other churches. It wasn't long before our pastor Gene Winfrey asked me to give him guitar lessons.

I played at church every time we had a service and Beverly played the piano. Meanwhile our church changed from Free Will Baptist to Southern Baptist and Gene went to Marietta, Georgia. We got a new pastor. Soon after arriving he came to me one Sunday after church was over and said, "I want to talk to you." He said, "I wish you wouldn't bring your guitar back to Church anymore." I asked him why. He looked at me and said, "Guitars belong in dance halls and beer joints." I looked right back at him and I said, "Yes Hoyt, mine has been in a few but I always believed it was sanctified the same time I was." I didn't take it back again. Almost everybody asked me why I quit playing my guitar. I just told them to ask Hoyt. It wasn't long before we changed churches and started to New Home Free Will Baptist in Berryhill. After a couple of weeks, the music director there came to me and said, "I know you play guitar, will you play a special for us next Sunday?" I said I would be glad to.

I had started building an electric guitar out of solid ash before we got moved into our house in Berryhill and finally finished it soon after. I put a two pickup on it and played it a while. My cousin Eddie wanted to buy it from me so I let him. Eddie was a dental technician and he drilled small holes around the entire body and fill them with the material used to make teeth with only it was red. It really dressed the guitar up. He played it for about fifteen years and sold it to someone else. About fifty years later he told me he saw that old guitar in a pawn shop in Bristow.

Later on I got a Fender Stratocaster guitar and played it for many years. When I was laid off for a while from American Airlines I was selling insurance and would go by the Fender warehouse over on I-44. Speedy West, the famous steel guitar player, was the manager and we would pick and grin for a little while when I had the time. Speedy kept asking me, "Why don't you let me order you a left handed Fender, I can get you a really good discount." They had to make a special order to get one made for a lefty. Speedy wrote many of the famous steel guitar songs, like Boot Heel Drag and others.

Later I bought an acoustic guitar and it is a beauty. I loved that guitar but soon after I had a mishap with my table saw and that ended playing guitar for me. I still have that guitar and just a year or so ago Tim Dunn was here tuning up Beverly's piano and I asked him if he would tune my guitar. I told him it hadn't been out from under the bed in twenty years. Tim said, "Oh wow, well, I'll try and see what I can do. Go get it." I brought it into the living room and he took it out of the case and being right-handed he finally managed to finger a chord and stroked it. He said, "How long?" All he had to do was tweak the little E a little. I guess it really liked its home under Melody's bed.

Grandpa's Stories

BOOT CAMP

On June 25, 1950 the Korean War, which started brewing a few years after WW II ended, became fact. The United States entered it immediately.

My close friends and I were too young to enlist in the military, so we waited. Finally, in January of 1952 James (Jimmy) Todd, Charles (Charley) Garroutte, and I decided to join the U.S. Navy. We got into my 1939 Ford Coupe and headed downtown to the Post Office which housed the recruiting offices. We went to the Navy recruiting office and were informed that there was a three month waiting list to join the Navy. We were really disappointed. We left there really feeling dejected. The very next office over was the United States Air Force. It was still being called the Army Air Corps. Charley said, "How would you guys like to be fly boys?"

I said, "Let's go in and check it out." They welcomed us with open arms. We told them that the three of us wanted to stay together; no problem there, they promised us. They said that we would be in San Antonio, Texas at Lackland Air Force Base by the end of the week. We signed the recruiting papers and were told to go back home and in a day or so, we would be notified to report to Oklahoma City for a physical examination and our induction into the USAF.

Three weeks later we were notified to report to Oklahoma City for our exams. We all passed our physicals with flying colors. In fact, one of the doctors told us if you could pee a hole in the snow you were fit enough for the military. While we were there, all of the draftees were lined up and asked to volunteer for the Marines and Paratroopers. They said they wanted five of each to step forward if they wanted to volunteer. About fifteen of them stepped forward. The Officer in charge said, "OK, you guys are Regular Army, and started pointing a finger at different ones: you, you, you, you, and you are Marines and you, you, you, you, and you are Paratroopers." Boy, was there some hollering going on. We were told to go

Grandpa's Stories

back home and wait until we were notified to return there, where we would be inducted and put on a train to San Antonio.

I received my notice on the 28th of February, to report there at 8:00 on the 2nd of March. By the morning of the 3rd I was at Lackland AFB, Texas. "THE GATEWAY TO THE AIRFORCE," "CENTER OF BASIC AIRMAN INDOCTRINATION," "HOME OF THE USAF OFFICER CANDIDATE SCHOOL." I was in Squadron 3705, Flight 394. There was not one single face that I could identify. Jimmy and Charley were nowhere around; I felt bewildered and was ready to go back to Tulsa, Oklahoma.

The first thing, we were fitted for uniforms and issued everything that we would need for Boot Camp. All my dress Blues fit like they were tailored to fit me. I wore 32x32 pants and a 42 regular coat, I was given a ID Card with my picture on it with all my stats, Height 5' 10 3/4", Weight 175, Hair Blond, Eyes Hazel. Boy, those days are gone forever. The first thing we did was box up everything we owned except our wrist watches, shoe shine kit, if we had one, and our tooth brushes, and wallets.

A few days later I found out Charley and Jimmy were there, but all in different outfits. The Air Force called them Squadrons. I told my TI (Tactical Instructor) Sergeant W. E. Roberts that I needed to see Captain Boatwright, our Squadron Commander. He asked what for, and I told him the Air Force had made a mistake. Charley, Jimmy, and I were supposed to be in the same outfit. He began to laugh. I said, "This isn't funny, Sarge Sir, they promised us that we could be together." He just kept laughing; finally, he looked at me, and said, "Airman, I really like you, we're going to have a great time here."

Grandpa's Stories

At the time we were in Boot Camp, the Korean War was at its hottest peak. They had cut our training period from 12 to 8 weeks. On our third day our TI was giving us a daddy talk. He said, "OK Airmen, they have only given me 8 weeks to make men out of you kids." (The oldest one in our Flight was 22 years old.) He said, "From this very second on I am going to be your mama and daddy, your best friend and your worst enemy." One of the guys from Louisiana (John Zumo) yelled back at him, saying "You ain't never gonna be my Mama or Daddy or Best Friend, I don't like your big mouth and I'd like to whip your A _ _." The Sarge just gave him a casual glance and told us to get into formation for a short march. He marched us to the field house, or gym as some called it. Inside, there was a full scale boxing ring where they held competition boxing matches. Sarge unlocked a locker and took out two pairs of boxing gloves. He tossed one pair to John Zumo and told him to put them on. He said, "OK big man, here is your chance to whip my _ _ _ if you can." Somehow I felt like John might have bit off more than he could chew. Zumo had already told a bunch of us that he was the Louisiana Golden Gloves State Champ and was second at the Tri-State level. At first I thought this would be a good match; on the wall were several photos of boxers, some holding trophies. I saw a couple of our TI; he was base boxing champion. Needless to say how that fight went. Zumo couldn't lay a glove on him. One thing though, Zumo could take a whipping. He wouldn't have survived the Sand Springs Line. Sarge could have killed him if he had wanted to. None of our bunch ever mouthed to Sarge again. I told Zumo afterward, "Hey Zumo, it's good you didn't grow up in my neighborhood." He said, "Why? Do you think you could take me on?" I told him, "Yes, John, with no trouble at all." We never had a reason to try though.

We had one guy from Fort Worth that didn't take a shower or change his underwear. He stunk like I don't know what. A couple of the guys went to Sarge to complain about him. Sarge told them for us to take care of that problem ourselves. He said, "Give him a good GI bath that he will never forget with scrub brushes and lye soap." About twelve of us were elected to carry this out. The guy tried to put up a fight, but soon found out it was useless. When we got through with him he was as red as a radish. He never missed a night of taking a shower from that time on.

One day after our evening chow, Carl Lord and I were the first ones to finish eating. As we walked outside the mess hall, the Oogie man was coming down the street. The Oogie man rode a three-wheel bicycle and sold ice cream, and had a Ooga horn on his bike. For those who don't know what a Ooga horn is, it's the kind of horn that was on the Model T and Model A Fords. Carl said, "Let's get us a fudgesicle, we can have it ate before the Sarge comes out, he was way behind us in line." So we both bought us a fudgesicle. About the time we turned around the Sarge was coming down the sidewalk. "Hold it right there," he said, "Who gave you two the permission to get ice cream?" In perfect unison, we said, "No one, Sir". "OK, put it in your pocket and you can have it when we get back to the barracks."

Carl had already removed the wrapper from his, but we stuck them in our side pants pockets. When the rest of our flight came out we fell in for our march back to the barracks. I could all ready feel the fudgesicle starting to melt and run down my leg. The Sarge took us the long way around and made us double time about three times which was very unusual after our evening mess. He usually figured we had enough for one day and would march us leisurely back to the barracks after our last meal of the day. When we finally got to the barracks, the Sarge dismissed and yelled out, "OK Layton, Lord, you can eat your ice cream now." Everyone in the flight knew why we had gone the long way and had to double time and they weren't very happy with us. There was nothing in my pocket but a dry ice cream stick; the fudgesicle had run down to my socks.

After about three weeks, our Squadron was assembled and a group of officers from Randolph AFB were trying to recruit volunteers for cadet training. Our fighter pilots were so outclassed by the far superior Russian-made MiG Jet Fighter Plane that it was bad situation over in Korea, we were losing pilots faster than they could be trained. They had lowered the

Grandpa's Stories

cadet training requirements from two years' college to high school diploma. They got a few volunteers; two weeks later they were back again; they had lowered the requirements to high school GED equivalent level. They got a few more that time. Carl looked at me and said, "Why don't we give this a try?" I said, "I'm game." That evening after the day's training was all over Carl and I went up to our TI's room and told him we wanted to volunteer. He looked at us and said, "Very gallant, but let me tell you what you weren't told today. Right now the life expectancy for a recruit pilot in Korea is 13 days." Carl looked over at me and said, "OK, why don't we sleep on this and we'll let you know tomorrow." It was never brought up again.

One day we were getting mass drill instruction. They had a Master Sergeant instructing us. We were sitting on a grassy little area on a hill side. A Flight of WAFs were marching by. Carl Lord kept turning around to look at them. When the Sergeant walked over to Carl and tapped him on the shoulder with a cane he carried, Carl turned around and said, "What?" The Sergeant said, "You like to look at those WAFs, don't you?" Carl said, "Yes Sir, I do." The Sergeant yelled at the WAF's TI and she called her troop to a halt. She walked over to our Master Sergeant and they conversed for a minute. He walked back over to Carl and told him to fall in with the troop of WAFs, and he marched around the block with them. He was somewhat embarrassed to say the least. When they came by again, no one even glanced their way.

On night I was on Guard Duty. I was guarding a group of four tents, my weapon was a three-foot hickory tent stake. About midnight I saw someone move in the darkness. I yelled for him to halt and he started running. I took in after him, we were just circling one of the tents when I switched directions. We almost ran into each other; he spun around and started the other way. I swung my stick hitting him across the leg between his ankle and knee. He fell and started screaming that I had broken his leg. I got my flashlight out to look at him. He was a Second Lieutenant.

About that time the Sergeant of the Guard come running up. "What's going on here?" he said. The Officer yelled back at him, "Your stupid guard here broke my leg, I want him court martialed." About that time, the O.D. (Officer of the Day) came running up. He asked what all the yelling was about. The Lieutenant told him the same story he had told the Sergeant. The O.D. was a Captain and he looked at me and said, "What happened here, Airman?" I told him how I had seen the Lieutenant and told him to halt. He then informed the Lieutenant that he was in a restricted area. He looked at the Sergeant of the Guard and told him to call the infirmary and have them come get the Lieutenant, and told me I had done my duty and to return to my post.

I had detail one day at the infirmary; my job was giving shots. There wasn't anything to it until my Flight came through. They saw who was going to give them shots and they were very upset to say the least. Our TI stepped up and said, "What's the matter with you babies? Layton is probably the most experienced one here at giving shots. He has given over a thousand shots today." After the first two or three they seem to settle down.

Boot Camp wasn't what you would call a fun time, but I really didn't mind it that much. It's something I think would help everyone to realize that they had obligations that they were responsible for. I did really enjoy the rifle range (you could qualify as Marksman or Expert. I qualified as Expert. The first five I shot at my partner's target, that helped him qualify as Marksman, but I still made Expert. I had been a good shot since I was 12.) and the physical training part of Boot Camp, because those were activities that I was good at. Some of the guys had never shot a gun of any kind, and I had grown up hunting and shooting all my life. To sum it all up, I'm glad I had the experience, but don't want to do it again.

CARL

Some of you knew and remember Carl L. Lord. Carl was born in Tucson, Arizona on December 22, 1934 and died November 25, 2001 in

Grandpa's Stories

Overgaard, Arizona where Carl was president of the local Veterans of Foreign Wars. His good wife Mary was the VFW Chaplain.

Carl Lord

I first met Carl at Lackland AFB in San Antonio, Texas. Carl had just gotten off a train from Tucson and I from Tulsa, Oklahoma. What attracted Carl to me was the pair of cowboy boots I was wearing. They were a very special pair of boots, custom made at a saddle and boot shop at our local stockyards: my first and only pair of handmade boots. I had on new Levi's with a hand tooled belt and a silver buckle set that my stepdad, Pop as I called him, had just made for me. Carl and I really hit it off from that very moment. When we were assigned bunks together, I choose the lower and Carl got the upper. We had guys ask us if we were brothers. One asked if we were twins. I was about a year older than Carl and I think he really trusted my judgment on a lot of things and looked to me as an older brother. We became best friends.

Some events in the life of Carl I wrote about in "Boot Camp." Those were the time Carl had to parade with the WAFs and the time he convinced me to get a fudgesicle.

After basic, Carl and I, along with several others from Flight 394, were assigned to A & P School at Sheppard AFB, Texas. I can recall Carl and I, Deane "Mike" Lawless, Jarel Florence, Sid Billingsley, Arthur Hard III, and Marvin Mills. Carl introduced us to Mexican food while we were at Sheppard. There was a restaurant downtown called the "Casa Manana" that Carl, Mike, Sid, and I ate at about every time we went to town. Until that time the only South of the Border food I had ever eaten was Hot Tamales.

One hot summer day Carl and I were walking back to the barrack from the PX. We were just about in the middle of the forty-acre Parade Field when softball size hail hit. We ran lickity split for the barrack with our hands over our heads. Carl had been hit on one of his shoulders that had almost driven him to the ground. When we reached our barrack, which

Grandpa's Stories

was across the street from the Parade Field, two of our guys were holding the door open and holding our field jackets and helmet liners and pointing back to the Parade Field. There was a guy down just about the middle of the field. Carl and I donned the jackets and helmet liners and headed right back into the hail storm. When we got to the guy he was really beat up and totally unconscious. We managed to get the guy up and onto our shoulders and proceeded back to our barrack. One of our guys had run over to the orderly room and told them what was happening. When it was all over, a Captain told Carl and I that we were heroes and would be commended for the act. They took the poor guy that was about dead to the hospital and we never heard any more about that incident.

When we were through with Tech School and everyone was getting their orders for their next assignments, about four or five of us were on the same orders going to gunnery school at Lowery AFB in Colorado. We were elated that we were getting to remain together. We cleared the base, turned in our bunks, and were waiting for finance to pay us and for transportation to the bus station in Wichita Falls when they came out and cancelled the orders for Carl and me. It was noon the next day before we were assigned to the 55th SWRS at McClellan AFB in Sacramento, California. We spent the entire evening and night without knowing what was in store for us and without a place to lay our heads.

There were way too many episodes while in the 55th to try and pen, but here is one I'll never forget. Carl and I were in downtown Sacramento one evening. We wandered into a place called the "Lion's Den." Bad name, right! We should have known better. I found a poker game and decided to try my luck for a hand or two. Carl started playing the little bowling games where you could win money according to what score you could post. I was hot that evening and couldn't lose. We had been there a couple of hours when I noticed that I was about $485 ahead. I told the guy over the game to cash me out that I had to get back to the base. I noticed the guy straight across from me give him the "no" sign. He said that policy was that the big winner could not just walk out on the game. He said I could leave without

Grandpa's Stories

my money. I said, "Sure, you can see me doing that." I saw Carl in a few minutes very nonchalantly stroll out of the building. My first thought was, "Carl, you can't just leave me here alone with these cutthroats." Then I realized that he had heard our conversation and was going for help. Fifteen or twenty minutes later Carl came back in with about six guys from the base and one of them was a guy we called Big Tex. Tex wore a size 57 jacket and was from New York City. He came directly over to me, picked the chair up with me in it and set me down about four feet from the table and bellered out, "Cash out, Layton, we got a bus to catch." The guy in charge didn't even look at the guy across from me but began to gather up my chips and cashed me out with about $525. We left that place without further incident.

Me with Carl in Alaska

While in the 55th Carl and I volunteered for duty in Korea, but were assigned to the 58th in Fairbanks, Alaska. One incident that I recall from Fairbanks, one night Carl and I and a few others were in Fairbanks at the Buffalo Saloon. Carl came over to me and asked if I had ever tried marijuana. I told him no way and he had better not try it either. He said a guy he met in there had some and wanted him to give it a try. A little while later another guy came over to me and told me that my friend was outside and was really sick. I went out and sure enough Carl was down on all fours puking his guts up. He looked up at me and asked me if he was going to die. I told him, "Yes, but probably not tonight." I got him up and went back inside and got a clean wet towel and cleaned him up a little and made our way to the bus station and went back to the base. Carl told me to never let him try anything like that again. I told him, "You dimwit! I tried to warn you." It turned out that a bunch of the 55th went to Alaska. There was Jim Buffalo, Ray Lowe, Darrel Hinton, Ken Waldron, Joe Komornic, Carl and I that I can think of. This same group minus Ken Waldron and Jim Buffalo and plus Ed Keenan all came back down the Alcan Highway together in November 1955. Two car loads. That trip is a story in itself. We stopped in Cheyenne, Wyoming, to let Carl off for a bus trip home to Tucson, Arizona, and Joe to Pueblo, Colorado. We all took photos and said our goodbyes. Carl came over to me gave me a big hug and gave me his address in Tucson; when we parted Carl had tears in his eyes. "Friends forever," I remember him saying. We all later were discharged from the AF and went our separate ways.

Carl and I continued to exchange letters. In 1957 Carl came to Tulsa and stayed for a week with us learning why we called Tulsa "Green Country." Carl had gone into the construction business with his father, Cal Lord, in Tucson. He married a beautiful girl named Mary. In 1961 Beverly and I took our children, Melody and Tommy, to Arizona to see Carl and Mary. Carl told me that he and Mary were unable to have children and had decided not to adopt.

When I decided to try and find the guys from my Basic Training Unit Flt 394 for a 50th Reunion, Carl was the first one I found. He and Mary were living in Overgaard, Arizona. He suggested we try to find some of our 58th guys and all get together as soon as possible. We had a Mini Reunion in 2001 with nineteen scheduled to attend. Carl and Mary failed to show although they had sent their check. Several of us tried to phone Carl with no success, we were afraid they had had an accident somewhere along the way.

After we returned home from the reunion, I tried calling Carl every day. Finally, after a day or two Carl answered, really sounding haggard. I actually thought he had been drinking. Carl said, "Connie, it looks like we will have to cancel out on the reunion. Mary is in the hospital and may not make it." I told Carl that the reunion was last week. He said, "Really, well I have been living at the hospital day and night." Mary died June 6, 2001. Carl told me that he had lost the love of his life, when he got everything back in order he would come and see us. I asked him if I could fly out there and spend some time with him. Carl told me not right then that he needed time alone to sort things out and figure out what he was going to do. Carl called me later from his brother's home in Honey Grove, Texas telling me that he had been there about a week and was getting ready to head back for Overgaard. I asked Carl to come up here a few days before he went home, but he assured me he had things at home that needed his attention. Carl's brother Stan called me right after Thanksgiving to inform me that Carl had passed away. Stan told me that after Mary died Carl quit taking all his medicines and that was what done him in. Stan sent me some of Carl's belongings, including his Basic Training photo. This aided me in finding some more of our Flt 394 guys. Carl had a few that signed his photo that had not signed mine. I really miss Carl. "Friends Forever."

AZORES

While visiting my daughter Melody and her family in Cleveland, Ohio, someone mentioned the Azores. I said that I had been there. Melody said she had been wanting to go there for years, and asked why hadn't I ever mentioned that I had been there. "Why don't you write a story about it?"

It was in August of 1953 and I was stationed at McClellan AFB in Sacramento, California in the 55th Strategic Weather Reconnaissance Squadron. We had one of our B-29s and its crew farmed out to an Operation called "Bootstrap." It was a thing of secrecy then, but now is common knowledge. They were photographing the whole continent of Europe and surrounding islands. This aircraft lost an engine and had to land at Lajes AFB on the island of Terceira, Azores. The Azores is a group of islands in the North Atlantic Ocean about nine hundred miles west of the coast of Portugal. My crew was selected to take a replacement engine and fly-way kit. A fly-way kit has all the tools and accessories needed to change out an engine on a B-29.

The B-29 was called "The Super Fortress." It was built during World War II but was still being used in the Korean War. The B-29 had two bomb

Grandpa's Stories

bays: forward and aft. The replacement 3350 Pratt Whitney Engine was loaded in the aft bomb bay, the fly-way kit in the forward.

Our trip was going very well until we lost our number four engine and had to feather it. The B-29 was considered to be an under-powered aircraft when hauling a full load, which we were. We were about halfway between Bermuda and the Azores when this event took place, so it would do no good to turn back. As we were losing altitude very fast our Aircraft Commander made the decision to salvo the load we were carrying. The bomb bay doors were opened and the salvo switches energized to release the engine and fly-way kit from the bomb racks. The kit from the forward bomb bay salvoed smoothly and fell to the Atlantic Ocean floor below, but the 3350 engine became cocked and hung up in the bomb bay. This was not a good situation to be in. The Aircraft Commander ordered me to look the situation over and make an attempt to dislodge the load and allow it to drop. I selected one of the radio operators to help me. I sent him down one side while I was on the other. While squeezing between the bomb racks and the outer skin of the fuselage the radio operator got his parachute hung up and panicked. I had to backtrack and go over and get him loose and settled down. Then we tried for about thirty minutes or so to shake the engine loose, but to no avail. If you have never been in the bomb bay of a B-29 flying with the doors open, you cannot imagine the noise level of those engines roaring and wind passing through. It was totally deafening and it took hours before my hearing returned to normal.

The Aircraft Commander ordered us back inside and attempted to do some maneuvers with the aircraft, designed to shake the bombs that had hung up on the bomb racks. That didn't work either. Our Aircraft Commander then offered our options to the crew and wanted input from every one of us. Our options were: Number one, bring all crew members to the front cabin and attempt to land, hoping that the engine would not dislodge on touch down, for if that happened our craft would surely break in two at the forward bomb bay area. Number two, bail out and abandon the aircraft. Number three, ditch the aircraft in the ocean, but the engine

Grandpa's Stories

could also dislodge and break the aircraft in half on impact. We discussed the fact that we were over shark-infested waters and immediately ruled that one out. The majority of our crew voted to land at Lajes AFB if we still had enough altitude to reach that destination. The Major ordered me to go back to the bomb bay and try to determine just how low the engine was hanging below the bottom of the bomb bay doors. Normally sitting on the ground there was about 12 inches of clearance from the ground or tarmac. I checked it and decided the bottom of the engine was pretty even with the bottom of the bomb bay doors. So we decided to try an emergency landing if we had enough altitude to reach Lajes AFB. We all had a laugh about our decision and agreed to buy the Major a case of beer if he didn't drag the tail skid. Our Aircraft Commander made the smoothest landing that I ever saw in a B-29, and I had logged over 1400 hours in those B-29s!

When our craft came to a complete stop, we deplaned in a hurry to see what it looked like. The engine had shifted some and there was about six inches of clearance between the engine and the runway. Everywhere you cared to look you could see emergency equipment set and ready in the event it was needed. We didn't need it. God had heard our prayers. The bomb bay doors were removed, jacks were put under the engine to level it and dislodge it. Next, the aircraft was jacked up high enough to get the engine out. The 3350 engine that we had carried over 6,000 miles had been saved and delivered to the aircraft it was intended for, but now we were stranded in a foreign land waiting for someone to bring us an engine.

We had lots of time on our hands. Lajes AFB had civilian mechanics that performed all work on the planes that came through there so we had nothing to do. After a few days some of us decided to go into the little town of Praia. I think the cab ride cost about 15 cents. It was a beautiful little town with lots of sidewalk cafes and such. The people were Portuguese and very nice. After walking around and looking the town over, we went into one of the cafes to have dinner. All the waiters wore black pants with short waist jackets like what we called an "Ike" jacket, white shirts, and little black bow ties. When our waiter came to take our order, I asked him if he

Grandpa's Stories

knew what a hot beef sandwich was. We couldn't read the menus because they were written in Portuguese. Our waiter could not speak English but he could understand a little of it. Very little. He nodded that he knew what I wanted.

Across the room I saw some people drinking what I thought was red wine from a very large beer schooner. I asked the waiter what they were drinking and he said red wine. I ordered one of those also. When our food was brought everything looked wonderful, but my hot beef sandwich looked nothing like what I expected. The meat was shredded and the potatoes were sliced into wedges and appeared to be deep-fried. The meat was resting on what I call French Bread and covered with brown gravy. The meat definitely was not beef, but I wasn't about to ask what it was. (It turned out to be very good.) When we all finished eating, he brought us all a tiny little cup of coffee, which we couldn't drink. You could have filled your ink pen with it and used it for ink. We asked him if we could have a beer instead. He brought us all a bottle of St. George beer in a green bottle. I had never seen beer in anything but brown bottles before. When we asked for our checks, we couldn't read that either. I pulled out a one-dollar bill, but he indicated change. I pulled my change out of my pocket, he looked it over and took a quarter and brought me back fourteen Portuguese coins, most of which were larger than the quarter I had given him. When I was informed how much money he had returned with, I calculated that my dinner had cost about twelve cents. At once I thought, "When I get discharged from the Air Force I'm coming back here to live."

Me during Flight

A few days later one of our other flight crews landed with our replacement engine. A couple of days after that the ground maintenance crew had our engine replaced and we were about ready to fly a test hop on the plane and get ready to go home. False! When we were doing the preflight test for the test hop, we found

53

Grandpa's Stories

that ground crew had put the wrong kind of fuel in our tanks and every fuel seal on the aircraft was leaking. Booster pumps, the banjo fittings on the fuel nozzles, every place you looked there was fuel dripping. We had to inventory and list every part that we needed new seals for and call our Squadron again for parts. After about ten more days we were ready to go home. We had flown a test hop and everything was OK. We had loaded our cargo, which was forty cases of Seagram's VO in forty ounce jugs. Liquor was duty free there and very cheap. $1.30 for a forty ounce jug. It was all for our NCO and Officers Clubs at McClellan AFB and a few select Officers and NCOs in our Squadron like Master Sergeant Donald Wilde, who was a survivor of "The Bataan Death March." Wilde was the man that taught me how to play Pinochle. We had several like him of World War II fame in the 55th at that time.

Well, luck was not with us. Operations grounded us because of hurricanes in the area. The next day, we learned that a B-29 and crew of eleven had bailed out of their aircraft and a search was in progress. If we wanted to join in on the search, we would be cleared for takeoff. We jumped at the chance. The downed crew was from one of our sister Squadrons, the 53rd Strategic Weather Reconnaissance Squadron from Bermuda, and some of our crew members had friends in that outfit. After about ten hours of searching, we received news that the survivors had been rescued and were on their way to the hospital at Westover AFB. There were four survivors. The others were lost, mostly to sharks. A few hours later we landed at Westover AFB.

When Operations at Westover designated where we should park our aircraft, we were met there by a unit of Air Police who set up a barricade around our aircraft and set to guard it and our precious cargo. Before we loaded in a truck, the Major instructed the guards that our aircraft was off-limits to anyone but our crew unless they had a letter from the President of the United States. We had figured that we would spend the night, refuel, and go home. Wrong! As soon as we were in Operations, the Major informed us that his mother and father lived in Holy Oak, Massachusetts, which was just down the road, and that that was his home town and we were going to stay three days. If any us needed any money, to let him know right now. Everyone agreed they were OK with money. Most of us never left the base.

After we had chow, we cleaned up and went to the hospital to see who the survivors were. None of us knew any of them. One fellow I was talking to told me that every time a shark approached him, he would kick or punch him in the snout. We went there every day we were there and sat with them. Some of us wrote letters for them to their families. On the third day the Major returned and we were ready to get on our way to Sacramento. When we got to our aircraft, one of the guards came over to me and asked what we were carrying that was so secret. I told him forty cases of Seagram's VO. He had the nerve to call me a liar.

Just as we were getting ready to leave, Operations ordered us to re-park for a little while. Air Force One had just landed with Dwight D. Eisenhower on board and no one could land or takeoff while Air Force One was on the ground. In about four hours we were notified that we were cleared and ready to leave. We had a very routine and uneventful trip back to Sacramento and were we glad to be home!

March 25, 2001

MY FIRST CRUISE

It was in November 1953. I had come to Parks AFB in California to be processed and to embark on a voyage to Alaska. I was being re-assigned to the 58th Strategic Weather Reconnaissance Squadron at Eielson AFB in Fairbanks, Alaska. I had been assigned to the 55th S.W.R.S. for the last year along with several buddies that had come from Sheppard AFB in Texas where we attended A & E (Aircraft and Engine) School after Basic Training at Lackland AFB, TX. Some of these buddies were Carl Lord, Darril Hinton, Ray Lowe, Joe Komornic, Ken Waldron, and Jim Buffalo. After being processed we were taken to San Francisco Bay to board our

Grandpa's Stories

cruise ship. It was the USS Thomas Jefferson, and already aboard was a Division of U.S. Army bound for Korea along with their heavy artillery, a few tanks, and war supplies.

Once aboard we were assigned tasks for the time we would be on the ship. Seven days we were told. Turned out to be nine. I drew a really tough assignment, "Guard Duty." This was standing guard over the female nurses' quarters. I had two shifts daily doing four hours at a time. The Navy Officer (2 bars like an Air Force Captain) that issued my piece and ammunition asked me if I could shoot anyone not authorized coming down my hallway to the nurses' quarters. I asked him whom would I be shooting? He informed me that there were probably more than a hundred soldiers on board that would do anything to keep from going to Korea. He said they would take my weapon away from me and use it on me, and it happens on almost every trip. I said, "I don't think so. This isn't my first time to pull guard duty. I'm not about to let anyone do that." He said, "OK, you will do." Would you believe two shifts twice a day for at least eight days and I never saw a female nurse, or a female of any kind? I never had to shoot anyone either. Praise the Lord.

Food wise, these Navy guys were a little off on their clocks. What I mean is they didn't know night from day. They served us beans for breakfast and oatmeal for dinner. I guess it didn't really matter much, for most of the guys didn't keep it down for very long. One thing I learned real quickly, after a meal, you don't go directly to the john or go on deck. One guy told me all he ate on the trip was soda crackers.

About the second day I was coming in from guard duty to our bunkroom when a Navy Chief came in and asked if anyone wanted to play pinochle. This guy had stripes everywhere, like an Air Force Master Sergeant with over 20 years. With him was a sailor with one or two stripes, I'm not sure. My buddy Carl Lord was lying there on his bunk in his shorts reading a Luke Short western. I said, "Well, if I can find me a partner I will play some." I said to Carl, "Hey buddy, do you play pinochle?" He said, "Yeah, I'll play with you if the stakes aren't too high." Carl got up and put his fatigues on. We spread out a blanket and the Chief got out his cards and started shuffling them. He said, "How about fifty cents a game and nickel a point?" I looked at Carl and he said, "That's OK by me." Carl stuck out his hand to me and said, "My name is Carl. What's yours?" I said, "Most everyone calls me Conrad." This Navy Chief and his partner played a pretty good game of Pinochle. What they did not know was that Carl and I were the "Base Pinochle Champions" of McClellan AFB where we had just left. We pretty well skinned the Chief and his crony. After we had removed $190.00 from them, the Chief said, "Just for the record, you two guys aren't really strangers are you? You guys have the best signals I have ever encountered. I know you do. We just never could figure them out." We never told them anything, just left them wondering.

It was a beautiful trip up to Seward, Alaska. Once there we boarded a very old train. It was a narrow gauge railroad like out of a John Wayne western. After all, this was still the Last Frontier and almost five years from statehood. It was a very scenic trip while it was still daylight. The train had to stop once to get a moose off the track. I can't remember exactly how long this trip took, but I remember eating the same meal three or four times, stew I think, and sleeping a little. The first thing I heard when we boarded was that gambling was legal now. It was dark when we reached Fairbanks and Eielson AFB.

SURVIVAL TRAINING

I spent two years in Fairbanks, Alaska while in the USAF. I was a flight crew member on B-29s with the 58th Strategic Weather Reconnaissance Squadron. Our Squadron flew two missions daily. The Loon mission departed at 0700 and the Ptarmigan at 0800. This took place every day of the year. You would really have to appreciate how hard and difficult it

Grandpa's Stories

was to get two B-29s in the air with the temperature fifty or more below zero. It was treacherous duty for the mechanics. Flight Crews flew every six days alternating between the Loon and Ptarmigan. Occasionally Special Missions would really mess up the schedule. Between missions we would fly Local Transition Flights around the Alaska Territory usually 4 hours, and test hops. The two regular missions were normally about 15 hours if everything went right. It didn't always happen that way. Some went as long as 18 hours, depending on wind streams, weather, and a few other obstacles. Our Ptarmigan mission consisted of 2832 nautical miles, three dimensional zig zag track that left Fairbanks toward the North over the Brooks Range toward Point Barrow and to the North Pole Basin and over three ice islands which we called T1, T2, and T3. The Loon track was 2896 nautical miles that left Fairbanks in a Southwesterly direction over Nome, Alaska and along the Siberian Coast to the point of the Aleutian Islands.

It was drummed into our heads that if we had to bail out, ditch, or crash land on the ice pack which was the Bering Straits we would have to survive on our own for 45 days or more. It was a daily part of our briefing before missions not to take survival for granted. At that time there was no such thing as long range helicopters. Our B-29s had a red tail section to make it easier to spot on the snow or ice.

About once every three months when we returned from missions there would be a six-by truck pulled up to our B-29 and the A/C would tell us to get our parachute and A-3 bag (this would hold my cigarettes, some food, some Tang, a hot toddy, some extra shorts, ammo, etc.) and load into the truck. They would take us to a point about 25 miles from Fairbanks. We would unload and they would give us the longitude and latitude that we had supposedly salvoed our three survival kits from the bomb bays, and tell us they would pick us up in seven days. The first thing we did was set up a camp and make

Grandpa's Stories

tents from our parachutes. Granted we were already tired from a very long mission but we put first things first. After camp was set up, our A/C would ask for all cigarettes and any food we might have in our A-3 bags. We would make a quick circle around the camp in hopes of locating one of the survival kit; we never did. After a night's sleep, usually about 3 or 4 hours, the commander would divide us into three groups to search for survival kits. I don't recall ever finding all three but sometimes we would find two of them. If we were that lucky we were OK. My A/C normally was Major George Cambridge who was the "A" Flight Leader or Capt. Nore Gustafson. I flew a little with Capt. Hiram P. Bilyeu and 1/LT John Yacalavitch, either way they would ration out the cigarettes about three a day and always put a guard on whatever food we had or could hunt down. He would make guard duty assignments, appoint cooks, hunters, camp workers (latrine duty). I was usually lucky enough to be a hunter, because I did it well.

Our survival kits contained a variety of what was needed to survive. At that time, it was the latest and best equipment. In each kit there was a First-Aid Kit and fishing tackle. Plus there were a number of weapons: 3 over-under pieces with 410 gauge on top and 22 calibers on bottom. They were not the fanciest weapons, but they would suffice to bring down a flying bird and kill some kinds of ground animals. I remember they had a wire stock and we had to assemble them. There was about 100 rounds of ammunition for each. We were always told that in the event of survival a lot of things were edible which we now hate to think of. In the event of us needing to go into survival mode, I would have been issued one of these and I would have been in charge of the security of the site since I was rated an Expert Marksman.

It was never a fun seven days, but it was necessary. When day seven came around, we would all be ready for our truck to show up. I'm truly thankful that we never had to practice it on the ice pack. We had lots of missions that barely made it back to base and some that crash landed along the coast line of Alaska.

Grandpa's Stories

OUR OLD 750 MAN BARRACK

Eielson AFB

I know a lot of you guys either lived or stayed TDY in this building at Eielson AFB at Fairbanks, Alaska. TDY means temporary duty. It was the home of the 58th Strategic Reconnaissance Squadron when I arrived in 1953, changed to the 58th Weather Reconnaissance squadron in 1954. I hope this story will bring back some really old good memories and not too many of the bad ones. I know I spent two wonderful years in it. (grin) Look in the lower right hand corner of the photo, this is our old barrack. Note the big hangar they were just building when some of us first got to Alaska in 1953 to the left and across the street.

This is how I remember this building, the one story jutting back behind the main building was the Mess Hall. I remember about 6-8 steps up to it from the first floor just across from our Orderly Room. The low building just to the left of it I do not remember at all. I'm positive it was not even there when I was there. The roads you see behind the building were added a lot later as well. This whole building was self-contained with a PX, armory, Airman's Club, laundry, and bowling alley in the basement along with I don't know what all. On the 1st floor near the Orderly Room was our mail room where we could pick up mail every day and also mail out things. I'm thinking our supply room was next to it. Our other Squadron Offices were also on the main floor. Second and third stories were personnel barracks. If you don't know what a PX is, it was like a modern day Walmart only smaller. You could buy almost anything that was needed like sporting goods, clothes, cigarettes, or snacks. You name it and it was there, and our prices were great.

You can see the two stairwells sticking up above the roof line. (Those are not elevator shafts. We didn't have any of those.) Quite a change since we were there. I remember looking out our third floor windows facing the west, nothing out there but 2 or 3 buildings. I remember the movie theater and Service Club being there, nothing else but boonies. Looking to the left you could see the new hangar being built. It was meant to house two B-36s. I remember the huge building across the street north of us was the Baker Field House and had just been completed. They named it after Charles Baker who was killed in the September 18 WB-29 crash just off the end of the runway. I spent a lot of time in there staying in shape. Flying long missions was really hard on the body.

When I first arrived we were still hot into the Korean War and the Cold War with Russia or Soviet Union, it was all the same. Russia had grabbed everything it could after WWII was over and formed "The Iron Curtain" around it. Eielson and Ladd AFB in Fairbanks and Elmendorf AFB at Anchorage, Alaska were considered to be the USA's first line of defense.

I remember you could get to the roof from the stairwells because I was up there once stringing copper wire for a radio antenna so we could pick up radio stations from the US. We were even able to pick up KVOO from Tulsa and listen to Johnnie Lee Wills. Also a little later Dan Ham threw a guy named Finkenberger off the roof. Didn't hurt him much; he landed in a snow bank.

But I am supposing that making such easy access to the roof was a defensive decision for us troops. That would give us the high ground advantage in case of an attack, though we never drilled for such an event. Also our personal issue weapons were in gun racks in each foyer between the bays where we could get them quickly if attacked. The foyers were very large serving all three bays coming into it to the stairwell.

Grandpa's Stories

Barrack

I'm thinking the guys were more or less separated by the job that they were doing. Off of the foyer where the gun racks were placed were huge bathrooms and showers that served all three bays. If you came to the far north door and to the stairwell and up to the 3rd floor you made a right turn and through the double doors into my bay. The first cubicle to the left was mine. I shared it with two other airmen most of the time. My cubicle had a desk in front of the window. I had my radio and a 45 rpm record player with a stack of records a foot high on it. This window was our refrigerator in the winter time. You could chill a case of beer really quick on the sill when it was 50 below zero. Each troop had a foot and wall locker. *See Editor's Note.

When I was there you parked right up next to the building so you could plug up your head bolt heaters so your car would turn over and start next time. (I didn't have a car, though I did have access to one many times.) It was a must. Head bolt heaters were nothing more than an electrical heater that had a few of the standard head bolts removed and replaced with heaters. They were just regular head bolts with a thermal unit inside with a wire coming out the top for plugging in. The heater would plug into any electrical outlet. You just needed a long extension cord to reach the outlets on the front of the building. All buildings up there had them. Most places downtown had outlets for their customers. If a car set very long without being plugged in, forget starting it again until it warmed up.

Our entry to the barracks was from the front only. We could enter any of the front doors at any time. Unless we were on a red alert. For the guys working on the flight lines and flight crews, you went out whichever front door was most convenient, made right or south to the corner then left or east to the flight line gate which was our entry to the flight line.

Birchwood Hangar

This put you at the Birchwood Hangar which was our hangar and it was the only one there at that time. In that hangar was our Maintenance Office, Operations Office, where we were briefed and de-briefed before and after missions. Our Radio, Radar, Electrical Shop, and some of the other service shops were also in there. We could get two of our B-29s in at the same time. Every evening the two B-29s selected for the next day's Loon and Ptarmigan missions were towed into the Birchwood. In the wintertime auxiliary heaters were hooked up to them to thaw them out enough to get into them next morning. Sometimes you could not even open the doors of the hangar because of the ice, snow, and cold. We would use the Coleman tractors that were used to tow our aircraft. It would usually get them moving.

Ninety percent of the tarmac also belonged to the 58th WRS. There were times we allowed TDYs to use it if needed. The 58th and one other squadron were the only flying units on base. Our fighter support all came from Ladd AFB downtown. The other unit was a photo reconnaissance group. With two RB-29s they used the west end of the tarmac and sometimes one of our nose docks and later the big hangar after it was finished. I'm pretty sure they lost both of those planes over Russia. I remember they disappeared one at a time. You had to have proper identification to get on the line and no cameras were allowed unless they were having an open house or something.

Grandpa's Stories

Nose Docks

The main gate was a mile and a half down that street you see running east and west. I remember our four nose docks straight south of the barracks had a door you could come out of to go to the barracks. Everything had six-foot chain link with barbed wire on the top. Our runway was two miles long--the longest in the world at that time. The tarmac ran almost that full length. If that street we used to get there had a name at that time it would have been Main Street. It was the longest street on the base. To go anywhere you had to use that street.

Probably none in our group can remember seeing green grass on the base. At least I don't and also not many trees until you got to the boonies.

September 2, 2016

*Editor's note: Melody has now had this footlocker in her continual possession for 10 times longer than Dad had it the entire time he was in the Air Force!

ALASKA IN THE COLD WAR

I arrived in Fairbanks, Alaska, Eielson AFB November 16, 1953. The Korean War was still going strong. There were two Air Bases located in Fairbanks (Eielson and Ladd), and one in Anchorage (Elmendorf). Eielson and Ladd were twenty-six miles apart. Ladd was almost downtown. Fairbanks and Eielson were at mile twenty-six on the Alcan Highway. My base, Eielson had one Battalion of Army Rangers guarding the installation. There were anti-aircraft guns set up all around the perimeter of the base. At least once a week we were put on Red Alert--meaning that some type of danger was lurking somewhere in the area.

Grandpa's Stories

We had the newest version of Tokyo Rose, she was Moscow Molly. She would play great American music from the 30s, 40s, and tell us about our latest beating and failures in the Korean War and what was new on Eielson and Ladd. I can personally guarantee you there were so many failures during that war it was sickening. The UN was calling all the shots and our generals were left twiddling their thumbs. Our bases in Alaska were considered to be America's first line of defense against any Russian or Chinese aggression. Everyone was issued a M1 Carbine which stayed in the racks in the foyer of our bays. Everyone who was on flight crews was issued a Model 1911 Colt Semi-automatic pistols which we kept in our footlockers or wall locker. When a person was assigned to do guard duty he would go out and find his personal carbine and load it.

During those alerts we were also called upon to do guard duty. Our 58th Strategic Reconnaissance Squadron had possession of the Birchwood hanger and four nose docks laid out along a one and one half mile stretch, and all that tarmac between for our parking and maintenance area. We had ten WB-29 Super fortress bombers converted over to Reconnaissance Ships and one C-47 which we were called upon to guard. There was a lot of sabotage going on I was told later. Once they found tiny cotton balls in some of the gas tanks on our WB-29s.

Me Sitting in the Right Blister Looking Out

I remember one morning we were getting ready for takeoff, the weather was terrible, ice fog and about 50 degrees below zero. Our radio operator turned on Molly, I heard her say, "You poor American Airmen getting ready to takeoff for your Ptarmigan Mission, I feel so sorry for you. You should still be sleeping. By the way your fourth runway light on your right side is burned out." When we started rolling I was looking at the lights as we passed each one, sure

Grandpa's Stories

enough the fourth was not lit up. It was obvious that she had spies there on base. On our runway the lights were located about every 100 feet apart down both sides.

Eielson AFB at that time had the longest runway in the country, designed for B-36 Bombers to land and takeoff. It always took more runway to take off than to land, especially when carrying a full load of bombs, fuel, etc. When I first got there they were in the process of building a huge hanger at the South end of the runway, big enough to house two B-36s at one time.

One cold winter night during a Red Alert one of our officers, a 1st Lt., was killed by an Army Ranger guard on our flight line. He was driving a weapons carrier going down the tarmac and the Ranger yelled for him to halt which he couldn't hear for all the truck noise. The Ranger cut loose with a BAR (Browning Automatic Rifle) and he ran over into a snowbank. I was always really leery after that because they always put a Ranger on our Birchwood Hanger and nose docks. One night I came in from a 16 ½ hour mission dead tired and as I was getting ready to get in the shower the CQ runner popped in and said, "Layton, you have guard duty in 40 minutes at nose dock # 4." I said, "Hey!! Wait a minute, I just came back from a mission." He just looked at me and said, "That's tough, talk to the first sergeant." It was almost 2:00 o'clock in the morning. I said, "Is he down in his office?" He said, "No, he is home in bed." He told me what the password was and I started getting ready for guard duty. A few minutes later when I approached nose dock # 4, I heard the breach on a BAR click, really something I was not wanting to hear. Then I heard, "Halt, who goes there?" I said, "A friend." The ice fog was so thick that I have no idea how he saw me coming, I guess he heard the crunching of my Bunny Boots in the crusty snow. I immediately started looking for him because I was not going down like the 1st Lt. did. He yelled out asking me for the password. My mind went blank and I said, "I just came in from a mission and I'm dead tired. I don't even remember what they told me." I was still trying to see where he was just to know the direction. About that time, I heard Joe Komornic say,

"Layton, is that you?" I said jubilantly, "Yes Joe, it's me." Then I heard the Ranger say, "Do you know this guy?" Joe said, "Yes, he's my best friend." The ranger said to approach slowly. I was one happy guy right then, I forgot all about being tired. My adrenalin was running sky high.

I remember that before I rotated back to the states two guys went out and got their MIs and blew their brains out. After the second one they removed the gun racks and kept all the carbines in the Armory which was downstairs on the first floor. I really don't know why they did that because almost everyone had a personal weapon of some kind. I had a 357 Magnum, a 16 gauge Ithaca, and a Remington 30-06. When I rotated back to the States I sold my 357, left the 30-06 with my roommate, and brought the shotgun home with me.

It only been since 1991 that it all ended. Today, just a little over sixty years, not everyone remembers the Cold War, the Berlin Airlift, or the wall Russia built splitting Berlin in half. (I knew a few guys that participated in the Berlin Airlift.) The Cold War ended in 1991 when Russia decided it was time to let the other countries in the Warsaw Pact go free and the Soviet Union was dissolved.

LOON AND PTARMIGAN

The Loon and Ptarmigan are both well-known birds of North America. These were also the names of the two missions assigned to the 58th Strategic Reconnaissance Squadron at Fairbanks, Alaska where I served in the USAF for two of my four years. It was 1953-55. At that time, we were flying WB-29s and in mid-1956 they went to the WB-50. As a matter of fact, all of our weather Squadron's missions were named after birds. I supposed Air Force and Birds go together.

Grandpa's Stories

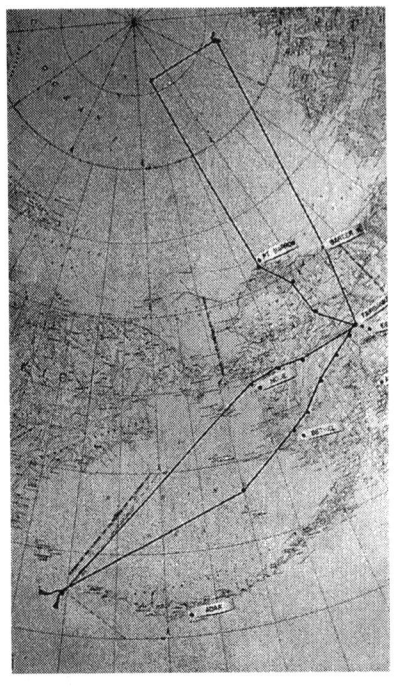

I remember the Loon was scheduled for takeoff first at 0700 and Ptarmigan at 0800. Both of these missions would average about 15 hours in the air. Tail winds and tail winds were the determining factor. The longest mission I ever flew was 18 hours and 7 minutes. When the engines were shut down after landing I could not measure any fuel in any of our fuel tanks. We must have landed on fumes and God's grace alone. Also our airspeed was determined by how many engines were still running we returned. Our rules were if you were to lose an engine on the outward leg of either mission it was cause to abort the mission. The same if loss of radio contact or of all cabin heat was to happen. Believe me when all cabin heat was lost the temperature would get to about 50 to 60 below zero in a hurry. Twice this happened to us. Coldest I ever saw was a mere 57 degrees minus zero. That was cold enough for me. Both times we had some bad cases of frostbite. I remember coming in from a Loon Mission and landing with only two engines still running. If this had been a Ptarmigan Mission, we would not have made it back over the Brooks Mountain Range. This map shows a good diagram of our routine routes.

Grandpa's Stories

Crew for 1000th Loon Mission—Layton 7th from left

We were often called upon to fly "Special Missions," always after our "bug catchers" had sniffed something suspicious, like Ionized Radiation. If the Special Mission was from the Loon Mission, it would be called Loon Echo. Always scheduled to take off at 0200. I cannot remember what the northern route Ptarmigan was called, <u>strange I flew many of them</u>. (Oh, well, I'm 80.) Note: 0200 is pretty early in the morning. It sure made for a long day. The Special Mission routes would always differ depending on USAF strategy.
2016

LIVE AMMO

It was early in the beautiful fall season in Fairbanks, Alaska. The year 1954, you could not ask for better weather than we were having for an outdoor bivouac. Someone had made the decision that flight crews needed more combat training in the event we were forced down somewhere in an undesirable, hostile community.

We were under the instruction of the U. S. Army Rangers that were protecting Eielson AFB from Soviet Union aggression. Eielson AFB was considered to be America's first line of defense during the Cold War. We were about 3-4 miles north of the base in the boondocks. They had an area cleared that covered about two acres of land with the cook wagons taking about a 50 foot square of it. That is where we went for mess. The rest was just open space. There were some bleachers set up for us to sit on while getting instructions from our ranger leaders.

Today was going to be a day of war. We were divided into two groups, the Red Army and the Blue Army. I was Blue. There were about 15 of us on

Grandpa's Stories

each side. We were issued 4 clips of 30 caliber ammo. We would all be shooting blanks to hold down the bloodshed. Our issue was our own M-1 Carbines from our squadron, the 58th WRS. We were all briefed and given stringent instructions and sent into the boonies for war. We were ordered to hold a certain position at all cost. Another guy and I were coming through the woods and I heard someone talking in a faint voice. I grabbed my companion by the arm and motioned to get down. About that time about five or six rounds were let go at us. I could hear the rounds tearing through the brush and a small limb fell and hit on my helmet. I immediately yelled out live ammo as loud as I possibly could. Just seconds later I heard loud yelling through a bull horn, "HOLD YOUR FIRE and assemble at the sound of my voice." We slowly, very slowly got up and went toward where the voice had come from. By the time we arrived most were already there. After the head count a 1st Lt. asked who yelled out live ammo. I said that I did. He then asked, "How did you know that there was live ammo?" I then said, "I could hear it tearing through the brush and a limb hit me on the head." He said, "Good enough." The Lt. said for everyone remove their clips from their weapon and make sure they take one out of the chamber. He told two guys to check every clip. Sure enough, one guy's had a clip full of live ammo. My first thoughts were Boy!!! Someone's head is going to roll over this. Our clips for the M-1 carbines held 30 rounds and he had fired 4 rounds. The Lt. then asked for all the extra clips and checks were made on them as well. He said, "OK, we're breaking for lunch while all this ammo is checked carefully. Be back here in an hour."

After lunch we had an uneventful war and my group lost. BUT!!! We learned a lot from those Army Rangers. Over the seven days of training we learned how to recognize booby traps and disarm them, how to win in hand to hand combat with the enemy, and the surest way to put a guy down. We even learned how to find eatable food about anywhere you are, but I don't want to make my readers sick. (grin)

Highlights of all this training were seeing all the different animals that came to our site to check us out and all the beauty of outdoor Alaska.

THINGS WE REMEMBER ABOUT ALASKA

* I remember that we had a "White Christmas" every year in Fairbanks. Our chance for a white Christmas in Oklahoma is less than 1%.

* I remember how long it took for our tires to round out after a cold winter's night.

* Do you remember the time the mess hall got the month's meat allotment and it was all hamburger meat? (1954-55) We were having hamburger fixed a 100 different ways and SOS every morning. One day I asked the Mess Sgt. if he had a thing for hamburger. He told me to get used to it because that was all they had. One hundred and twenty-five thousand pounds of it. Some of the guys got so tired of it that they started eating C-Rations.

* Yes, I also remember the green eggs. I decided they weren't so bad if you put enough catsup on them.

* Anybody remember the 1st Sgt. that walked with the big cane. I found out later that he was the sole survivor of a barrack fire in Japan, he was one tough guy.

* I learned really quick not to try and loosen the metal buckle on my gloves with my teeth when I came in from the outside cold. (BRRRR!!!!)

* Do you remember how easy it was to chill your beer in the winter?

* I remember paying $4.80 for ham and eggs at the bus station in Fairbanks, but boy were they good.

* I remember the "Oogie Man" that came around every evening with all kinds of goodies in his truck. I saw guys waiting in line with just shorts and shower clogs with the temperature below zero. Crazy, huh?

* Roger "Pockets" Cole reminded me of how good the snow shoe rabbits were that I would cook and share with the guys.

* I remember "Stud" Colburn going into the burning liquor store that was next door to Moose Creek Lodge when it burnt down and coming out with an arm load of booze, singed eyebrows, and black all over.

* I remember killing 12 mosquitoes with one swat of my hand. Were they thick or what?

Grandpa's Stories

* I remember mailing home 250 Silver Dollars just before I rotated. They never got there. (groan)

AN UNFORGOTTEN DAY

Breakfast for Loon Mission--Layton in rear

It was the winter of 1954-55 and one of those dark, cold winter mornings when you couldn't cut the ice fog with a knife in Fairbanks, Alaska. My crew was scheduled for what was called "Special Mission." The 58th Strategic Weather Reconnaissance Squadron routinely flew two weather missions daily out of Eielson, AFB: The Ptarmigan and Loon Echo. Takeoff time for this "Special Mission" was 2:00 a.m. which meant the Flight Crew had been up for about four hours getting ready for this Mission, starting with a really good breakfast, briefing, preflight, etc. When everything went well, this mission was about 24 hours bed to bed with about 15 to 18 hours in the air. Usually things were pretty routine and went very smoothly. There were 12 Flight Crews in the 58th, divided into 3 Flights, A, B, and C, with crews numbered 1 thru 4. My crew was # 1 Crew in Flight "A", our Aircraft Commander was Major George R. Cambridge. The Major was also over all of Flight "A" and was the Squadron's Chief Operations Officer. The Major had flown bombing missions over Germany during WWII. He was one of the finest men I've ever known. There being 12 crews meant that we flew routine missions every six days, always alternating between Loon and Ptarmigan except when there was a "Special" scheduled in. This was usually after the previous day's mission had encountered new Russian nuclear activity and more additional information and monitoring was needed.

Briefing for Loon Mission—Layton on left

All flight crews didn't fly the "Specials." It was my understanding that only Flight A was briefed for flying these, why I don't know. We also flew what were called Locals or Transition flights and test hops in between. I hated flying test hops because that meant flying with Major Luther J. Miller, our "Maintenance Officer" for the 58th Strategic Weather Reconnaissance Squadron. Major Miller was an extremely hard man to please; he was a survivor of the Bataan Death March during WWII. I heard many times that he was so tough that he could stare down a WB-29 that wasn't running to suit him. I loved flying the Transitions in the summer time because it was always light and you could really see the beauty of Alaska, "The Last Frontier." At that time Alaska was just a territorial possession of the United States and not yet a state. These Transition flights were not just pleasure flights. We were in a "Cold War" with the Soviet Union and we were actually monitoring the area around the most "Strategic" area in Alaska, Eielson AFB. We knew there were Soviet spies in the area because Moscow Molly could tell us on her radio program when we had a runway light out or if the fog was too thick for us to safely fly our missions. She would often try to discourage us from taking off.

Well, I kind of strayed off the story so let's get back. This appeared to be just one of those routine missions that usually go very smoothly. We were about seven hours into the mission when I noticed that the navigational lights on the right wing had gone out. I called the A/C to see if someone in the cockpit had inadvertently hit the switch that turned them off. He said,

Grandpa's Stories

"No, I just now turned them off, prepare the crew back there for silent operation. Layton, you know the drill. Two of the Navigators are on their way back now." "What did you say?" Then I said, "Sir, I said #%*&, but I didn't think I said it loud enough for anyone to hear on the intercom." The Major said, "We'll talk about that in the de-briefing room when we get back." What this meant was that we were going to take a little side trip that wasn't always a part of our special missions. We had done this on two other occasions. It meant that for safety reasons the extra two navigators and the weather officer would come to the rear compartment. Everyone was strapped in good and tight. It also meant a possible 3 to 4 hours in de-briefing, a rather lengthy check for radiation levels on the ship, checking our dosimeters, our bodies, and clothes, and possibly having to burn everything we were wearing and everything in our A-3 bags. This had happened the last time we did this exercise. I got up to notify the Drop-Sound Operator that he would not be making drops for the next couple of hours and the Radio Operators to reel in the radio antenna and to monitor, but to maintain radio silence and for the extra Operator to move to the bulkhead with the Navigators. We would be lowering our altitude for low level flight to try and avoid radar detection and I wouldn't be using the Altus lamp during this period. The Altus lamp is a hand held spotlight with about 2 million candle power that will shine several miles on a clear night.

    Well, everything seemed to be going smoothly. I was leaning out in the right blister trying to see anything that might have come into view when, wham, bam, our right wing tip hit something, sparks flying big time, but only a slight jolt had been felt. The Major broke radio silence, to me he said, "What in the hell was that?" I said, "Sir, our right wing tip just hit something, we must be awful low." The Major asked, "Can you see any damage." I said, "Major, I can't see anything but dense ice fog and that means we are almost on the ground. Do you want me to use the Altus lamp?" Then the Major says, "#%&*!" About that time, I could feel the power being applied and we began to climb, but too slow to suit me. After a few minutes the Major told me to use the Altus lamp and look over the right wing. I did and couldn't see anything wrong. The Major said, "What do think we could have hit?" I told him it could have been a radio tower, a tree, or maybe another plane, maybe some kind of ground fire. All I saw were the sparks like we struck something metal. The Major then told the Navigator to chart exactly where he thought our location to be when we felt the jolt. The Major then said, "OK, we are getting back on track now, but keep radio silence for another 30 minutes. Layton, you keep your eyes on that right wing, if you see anything wrong I want to know immediately. Whatever we hit has really affected the trim."

Within 45 minutes we were back on track and completing the mission. Everything went pretty routinely with the exception of the trim on our aircraft; it appeared we had an excess amount of drag on the right wing. When we landed at Eielson everyone was very happy to be back on the ground. When we had taxied back to the tarmac, we had a welcoming committee waiting for us. There was Major Miller, Col. Morales, C/O of the 58th, and transportation to take us to Operations for de-briefing, and as always Team 202 to check us for Ionized Radiation. On our inspection of the aircraft, the right wing tip had definitely struck something and was heavily damaged. I was standing there shining my flashlight on it, when Major Miller walked up beside me and very nonchalantly said, "This did not happen in flight. This aircraft hit something while taxiing. We'll decide just what and when we get to de-briefing." (It was decided that our wing tip hit another one of our B-29s parked on the tarmac as we were taxiing to park the aircraft.)

I was right about being in de-briefing for a long time. We also checked hot for radioactive materials and everything we had on board had to be destroyed, including a carton of Camels and two new Luke Short Westerns I had in my A-3 bag. To this day I have no idea just what we hit that damaged the wingtip on that mission, but that was the last "Special Mission" I flew while on my tour of duty at Eielson.

Grandpa's Stories

There were plenty of other times when I was just as concerned. Once on a routine Loon mission I overheard the Navigator say to the A/C, "Major, if my latest calculations are correct we are more than 250 miles into Siberia." Now you talk about a fast turnaround, we made one. We were expecting to encounter MiG fighters at any time and that was not a pleasant thought. I had looked at a few MiG pilots in the eye but never over Soviet territory, we had always been over international waters. On one occasion while flying missions, I was looking eye to eye with a young pilot in a MiG 15. I notified my A/C and asked if I should give him the finger or salute him. Maj. Cambridge asked, "Can you tell what rank he is?" I said no. The Major said, "Well, let's not provoke him," so I gave him a salute. He grinned at me and lifted straight up out of sight. This was just a short time after the Russians had shot down one of our Navy PBs near St. Lawrence Island, which was on one leg of our Loon mission.

I remember on a Ptarmigan mission we were still in international air space and it was very dark and cloudy but I kept getting a glance of navigational lights far below us. Capt. Nore Gustafson was the A/C. I reported it to him. He told me to keep watch on them. We were probably only two minutes back into the Alaska ADIZ (Air Defense International Zone) when I saw a bright flash below us and a fireball falling to the ground. This was more than likely a Soviet aircraft trying to slither into Alaska under our wing trying to evade radar. They were intercepted by a pair of F-89s that always came out to intercept us as we re-entered our ADIZ.

Once after completing a Loon Echo mission, I was installing the down locks on the bomb bay doors and discovered some bullet holes in the doors. Upon checking the aircraft, we found 17 bullet holes in the underneath side of our B-29 which appeared to be from small arms fire. We had never known when it had happened.

Well, I could probably go on with little blips of memory like this. Those were some of the days bored into my memory that I shall never forget. CRL

Grandpa's Stories

Note: The 58th at this time was disguised as a weather squadron which was partly true, but the main purpose was to monitor Russia's nuclear program. All flight crew were cleared for "Top Secret" security and everything we did was Top Secret at that time. We were all sworn to never speak about any of our flights. Even the mechanics and ground crews did not know what we were doing. In 1977, it was revealed in *Time Magazine* what we were doing during the Cold War with the Soviet Union. The "oath of secrecy" was lifted in 1996.

DOWN THE ALCAN HIGHWAY

It was November 16, 1955, when we departed good old Eielson AFB Fairbanks, Alaska. We had all seen two extremely harsh winters and were well into the third. We had seen temperatures of up to 57 degrees below zero. We had been assigned to 58th Strategic Weather Reconnaissance Squadron for exactly two years. That is all except Ed Keenan. Ed got an unwanted extension for 30 days.

Carl Lord, Ed Keenan, me, Ray Lowe, and Darril Hinton (in car) Cheyenne, WY, November 1955

As I recall it was a pretty day for November and we were all really excited about being on our way home after two years in this wonderful place. We were a two car caravan getting ready for a 4400 mile trip down the Alcan Highway, Darril Hinton's 1951 Mercury and Ray Lowe's 1954 Ford. 1400 miles of this highway through the Yukon and Canada was gravel road. Darril had sent his Peggy home to Sabetha, Kansas and Ray had sent Dee back to South Dakota. Carl L. Lord, Ed Keenan, and I were riding with Darril and

Grandpa's Stories

Joe Komornic was riding with Ray Lowe. Carl Lord and I both were proud owners of really long "handlebar mustaches." They were almost a full year of growth.

Both cars were loaded to the gills with our luggage and everything we owned along with all the spare parts and extra gasoline that we could safely carry without blowing out all the tires. I had gone to the post office and mailed home a box with 250 silver dollars and a Carters Little Liver Pill bottle full of gold that I had spent two days panning for. However, that box never reached Tulsa, Oklahoma. Someone made a little extra that day. We went to the bank at Eielson to convert our American money over to Canadian money to simplify things as we came down through Canada. The Bank told us that both Canada and the US currency were exactly the same and would not change for at least two to three weeks. Not so-- everywhere we stopped after we left Alaska we took a 10 to 20% hit on our American money. These people were not crooks but just took every advantage of us that was allowed by law.

We were in the Yukon before we had any kind of problem. We were following an eighteen wheeler (semi-truck) through new snow letting him make ruts for us to follow when all of a sudden he stopped, got out and came back to our car and said, "Are you guys following me?" We said, "Yes, as long as we can." He said, "Well, you are going to have to back outta here because there is a barb wire fence in front of me." The driver had gotten off the highway without even knowing it. We all backed up about two or three hundred feet when he took off again. We still weren't sure we were on the highway until about a half mile on down the road we passed a mile marker.

When we entered Canada we had to stop at customs and declare any weapons we had and to have them sealed. Keenan had a 22 pistol and I had an Ithaca 16-gauge shotgun. I had sold my 357 Magnum pistol before leaving Eielson. I remember buying that 357 at the PX for $87.50 and when I sold it, the same gun was selling for $125 and the guy offered me $100 for it and my holster. I also had a Remington 30-06 which I left with

Grandpa's Stories

the guys in my room because it had been given to me. They told us that customs would check to see if any seals were broken on our guns. And if so we had better have a very good reason.

We were well into Canada and I was driving, Carl Lord was riding shotgun, and Darril and Ed were sleeping in the back seat. It was dark and I hit a huge mountain lion. Carl said, "Stop the car, I want to cut that thing's head off and have it mounted when I get home." I didn't stop and I told Carl he was crazy. I said we may not have killed that cat and if he's still alive he would be mighty pissed at us. Carl grumbled and moaned about it but we kept right on going down the highway.

A little farther down the road we had to stop and Darril changed the brushes in the generator. I had never seen anyone change brushes as fast as Darril did, maybe it was because it was about 30 below zero. Later Ray ran out of gas but luckily we had some extra, so we were all able to get to the next gas station. In that part of the country the gas stations were many miles apart. That is why you had to carry extra gasoline if you were driving straight through. On the Alcan Highway the cost of gasoline averaged about 78 cents a gallon and we thought that was very high, even though their gas was measured by the Imperial gallon which was five quarts rather than four. I remember we pulled into one place early in the morning before it even opened for the day. We sat in the drive for a couple of hours before they opened. It turned out to be worth the wait as the guy's wife fixed us all a really good breakfast of ham, eggs, and pancakes. It felt really good to be out of the car for a little while.

Ray's 1954 Ford broke a fan belt somewhere between stops and we took him to the next gas station and all they had were used fan belts. In the back of the building there was a pile of fan belts about three feet high and about eight feet in diameter. The guy told us to pick out the one we wanted. Ray had his broken belt and found one he thought would work. The guy charged Ray 12 bucks. I told him I thought Jesse James was dead, but he said we could take it or leave it. Ray gave me a stern look and said, "I'll take it." A little farther down the road Ray's water pump went out. We were in

Grandpa's Stories

a pretty small town and the guy running the garage told Ray he didn't have time to do it but he would order the water pump and loan us the tools and place to fix it ourselves. We had to wait about two or three hours for the pump, I can't remember the cost of the pump but it was three or four times what it would have cost at home and he charged Ray $20 for the use of his tools.

When we got to Edmonton, Canada we were starting to smell pretty rank so we stopped and got a room at a motel and all took a shower and changed over to regular clothes (Levis and shirts). Laying on a real bed while we were waiting sure felt good.

Somewhere south of Edmonton we hit what the locals called a "Chinook." That's a warm wind blowing and melting the top layer of ice. It was almost impossible to stay on the road; we drove about 10 to 15 mph until we got out of it.

When we pulled into customs at the Alberta and Montana State line the guy up north turned out to be correct. They did check to see if any seals were broken on our weapons. It felt very good to once again be in the USA. Especially after we got to Great Falls, Montana and points further south. We pulled into Cheyenne, Wyoming about noon and pulled into a bank parking lot, just across the street from the bus station. It was about 30 degrees and there were a lot of people moving about. They were bundled up like it was really cold. We were in blue jeans and shirt sleeves. They thought we were crazy. We told them that we had just come from Fairbanks, Alaska and thought this was great weather. We were making some changes with our luggage and stuff. Carl Lord was going to take the bus from there to go home to Tucson, Arizona, Joe Komornic was headed home to Pueblo, Colorado. Ray was going to make a bee line for South Dakota as fast as he could to see Deloris again. We had been on the road for a little more than four full days.

The parting of all us guys was pretty emotional, we had all been very good friends for a very long time. Carl was my best friend, we had met on the first day of basic training at Lackland AFB and had never been parted until now. Ray Lowe, Darril Hinton, and Joe Komornic were on the same orders sending us to the 55th at McClellan from Sheppard AFB, Texas where we went to A & E School. I was Darril's Best Man when he married Peggy in Sabetha, Kansas in 1953. While at McClellan Ray, Darril, Joe, Carl, and I always ran around together. They were like brothers to me. I met Ed Keenan about the second day I was in Alaska. He was already a friend of my roommate Paul Davis and came to our cubicle often. Especially when we had a case of beer! A lot of guys just happened to drop in about that time. I think they could smell it. It was a sad parting for me as these guys had been my best friends and all were really great men. At that time, I didn't know if I would ever see any of them again.

When we got to Omaha, Nebraska we took Ed to his sister's house and he later took a bus to Fonda, Iowa, and we turned south for Sabetha, Kansas. Upon arriving at Sabetha, Darril took me to his folk's house where I spent the rest of the night and he headed for Peggy's house. The next morning, I took a bus home to Tulsa, Oklahoma. I can truthfully say that it was a trip to remember! When someone tells me they drove up or down the Alcan Highway, I think to myself, been there and done that! But it does bring back many wonderful memories.

At the time of our departure Alaska was called "The Last Frontier." If you were there at that time you know the reason why. January 3, 1959 Alaska became the 49th star on our Great American Flag. Since that time many of my friends and guys coming to the reunions have made the trip back up there and shared their stories and photos of the changes that have occurred in Fairbanks and Eielson AFB over the years. A lot of these changes can be seen in our reunion program that I hand out every year. I love hearing these stories and viewing the photos but I have never had a desire to return to Alaska. Like I said in the story, been there and done that.

NOTE: It has been almost 55 years since we made this trip. I'm sure I have forgotten some of the highlights of the trip. I may also have some of the facts slightly distorted.

Grandpa's Stories

We lost Carl Lord in 2001 and Joe Komornic in 2008. I really miss both of them.

August 13, 2010

33RD AIR DIVISION TINKER AFB, OKLA CITY, OK

When I returned to the US from the 58th WRS in Fairbanks, Alaska in November of 1955, I was stationed at Tinker AFB and assigned to the 33rd Air Division. We were the Headquarters Squadron for the whole division of B-29s and B-50s that were strung out over about seven different air bases. We were a small unit just east of Tinker AFB, a place called Cherry Hill, sometimes Cherry Hump. Our mission was to detect, intercept, and destroy. This task was done by three hundred plus WAFS and 38 Airmen and Officers. We had one hangar on the Tinker flight line, two T-33s, one B-25, which was the Commanding General's personal aircraft and one C-47, which I was assigned to as Flight Engineer. At Cherry Hump there were about eight barracks: seven for WAFS and one for airmen with the lower floor used as a day room. There were also a few office buildings and a mess hall. The mess hall was like walking into an Officers' Club on most bases I had ever been on. You could order almost anything you wanted and tell how you wanted it cooked. There was a large conservatory and a Radar Dome stood at the back of the little village. I never knew exactly what was done in it.

My duties included being load master and radio operator, figuring weight and balance, loading enough fuel for our flight plans and getting the officers coffee on occasion, although most waited on me. I did pre-flight and post-flight and ensured that all maintenance was done properly. Sometimes we were assigned to pick up faulty radar and electronic equipment all over the US and take it to repair stations or to haul the WAF basketball team to wherever they were playing at the time. One interesting monthly assignment was taking a "Special Services Unit" from

Grandpa's Stories

Norman, Oklahoma for their monthly parachute jump. Another "tough" job was hauling base VIP's to special events like the Rose Bowl Parades.

I never saw the Commanding General fly his B-25 but on four occasions I had the privilege of flying with him in the C-47. When that occurred I was treated like royalty everywhere we went. I would eat with him, sleep in the same quarters, and I never had to refuel or do anything to our ship. He had everything taken care of. The General told me on one occasion, "Sarge, I never like to be separated from my crew. We never know when we may have to scramble." He always asked me about my girlfriend. When I came home from Fairbanks on leave I had met Beverly.

I had been writing to her for a couple of months and she just happened to be in our dining room under the pretense of using our encyclopedias for her homework. She was a senior in high school. I thought she was about the most beautiful girl I had ever seen so I decided to try and get a week extension on my leave.

I called Tinker AFB and asked to talk to the Commander of the 33rd Air Division and Brigadier General William Preston Nuckols was put on the line with me. He listened to what I was trying to do and said, "Airman, I don't think I can help you. How did you come to call me?" I said, "General, all my orders say is 33rd Air Division and I thought I would need to talk to the commanding officer to get an extension." He said I was probably assigned to Headquarters Squadron and he would have me connected to Captain Hill, the CO. When Captain Hill came on the phone the first thing he asked was why was I talking to the General Nuckols. I told him the same story that I just told the General and he told me to take whatever time I needed. After I cleared in to Tinker my first flight was with General Nuckols. He came over to me and said, "Hi Sarge, I saw your name on the itinerary. Did you get leave extension you were wanting?" I told him yes.

Grandpa's Stories

We were friends ever since. I really liked General Nuckols and enjoyed flying with him.

I wasn't in the 33rd very long but I logged almost 200 hours in that little "Goonie Bird." I actually got to sit in the pilot seat on a couple of occasions and fly the plane. Being in the 33rd was a little different than flying the WB-29s in the 58th WRS at Eielson. We flew all over the area from Chanute AFB, Illinois and as far as California. I really enjoyed the times we took the Special Forces guys for their monthly jumps. There were sixteen of these Special Forces guys: four Navy, four Air Force, four Marine, and four Army Rangers. Their commander was a Marine Captain. There was a target painted on the ground over by the University of Oklahoma at Norman where they were all based. We would make a pass over it and they would jump in groups of four. On one occasion an Army Ranger Staff Sergeant was lined up third to jump and when his time came he froze in the door. The Captain grabbed him by the arm and yanked back and told him to get in the next group. He was third again and same as before he froze in the door. The Captain yanked him back again and told him to lead the next group out. He did that without a hitch. When they were all out I asked the Captain what happened to him. He told me he had no idea; he had made 27 jumps already and had never landed in an airplane.

The WAFs were a mess to deal with. I hated hauling them around. They would argue about who was going to sit where. A few times I took the bull by the horns and assigned them a place on one of the benches. They would grumble and gripe but wound up doing what I said. I hated cleaning out the "honey bucket" after a flight with them. Honey bucket was what we called the toilet in the rear of the aircraft that wasn't enclosed by anything. They always filled it up with toilet paper and bloody kotex. They would just throw their trash on the floor.

On the other hand, picking up radar equipment all over the country was really interesting. We would go to places like Chanute, Texarkana, Fort Worth, and many other air bases all over the country. We would take most of it to Kirtland AFB in New Mexico. When we would go to Love

Grandpa's Stories

Field in Fort Worth I would sit and watch Navy flyers trying to land on an Aircraft Carrier deck, which was painted on one of the runways. The guy that tried to direct them with his flags would have to jump in a hole every once in a while. I loved that duty; it sure beat flying the 16-18 hour missions out of Alaska.

We had one really exciting episode while in the 33rd. We were returning from a base in California. Over Amarillo, Texas, we were in a very turbulent storm which is always typical over that town. I was sitting at the radio trying to get weather updates. All of a sudden we hit an air pocket and must have dropped at least 50 feet in about a second. I don't really know how the old aircraft even was able to withstand such a move. The seat I was in was on a pedestal mounted to the floor. It broke loose and all of a sudden I was back thru the wall separating us from the rear cabin and cargo area. I was slammed all the way to the back of the ship. When I came to my senses I realized I was almost on top of the APU (Auxiliary Power Unit) at the rear end. At first I thought we were going down, then I realized we were going up at a very steep climb. I unstrapped from the seat I was in and started forward to see what was happening. Our climb angle was at least 12 degrees or more and it was a difficult crawl to get back to cockpit. When I finally got there the pilot and co-pilot were fighting over the controls. The pilot was pulling back and the co-pilot was pushing the controls. It didn't take me very long to assess the situation. I grabbed the pilot by both shoulders and started shaking him as hard as I could. I was yelling in his ear to get a grip on himself and ease up. With the adrenalin he had flowing he was super strong. Finally, he eased up and the co-pilot was able to start levelling our flight. When it seemed that the Captain had come to his senses he turned to me and told me to try to make radio contact with the AFB at Amarillo and see what we were showing on their radar. We had climbed over 5,000 feet and he started to lower our altitude again. I was able to make contact and they were wanting to know if we were OK. I went back to the Captain and said, "Captain, come on back and I'll get you a cup of coffee." He agreed. I let down one of the bench seats just behind the bulkhead that I had just broke and sat him down, then I got us both a cup of coffee. We just had a casual talk for a few minutes and he said, "I'm OK now." He got up and went back to his duties. In a few minutes the co-pilot came back and sat down by me. He said, "Sarge, what are you going to put in your report?" I said, "Lieutenant, we hit a wind shear in the storm and it played hell with our ship." He looked at me and smiled. He said, "You know Jack flew over 57 combat missions over Korea. I think he just thought he was back there or something." I said, "No telling, but he's OK now. I'll fly again with him."

When it came time for my discharge, Captain Hill called me into his office and tried to get me to re-enlist for another four years. He promised me a staff position within a month if I did. I told him if he would put that in writing I would consider the proposal. He said, "You know I can't do that." I said "Sir, that is exactly why I am getting out. I should have made Staff six months ago." I was discharged on March 3, 1956.

WB-29 # 214

The year 1953. I was assigned to B-29, tail number 4-62214. This is a ship with a very long record, the first aircraft to discover that our "Cold War" enemy Russia was experimenting with nuclear power. Now it is a tourist attraction in a shallow lake on Eielson Air Force Base. It is called "The Lady of the Lake." I have written several stories about this aircraft and explored many views on what actual aircraft it really was. I'm not going to repeat all of these yarns because most are guessed at, and some are made up, I think. (grin) The facts were discovered in August 2013 when a team from Eielson, conducted by a Government historian, led a photo reconnaissance dive into the lake to look for data plates. Their goal was to verify exactly what aircraft this actually was. They found the data plates and retrieved one wing that had fallen off and confirmed it was old # 214. I knew that all the time as I believed the stories told to me by people I trusted that were still there after I left Alaska in 1955.

Grandpa's Stories

Two years ago, not long before our Air Force reunion in Branson took place, I received a package in the mail from a friend, Major Bernie Houle. Bernie was a pilot in the 55th WRS at McClellan AFB where I was prior to going to the 58th in Fairbanks, Alaska. Bernie was also one of the pilots who participated in the atomic experiments at Eniwetok atoll in 1953. I had to work on those B-29s that were "hot" as all get-out. From the IRR (ionized radiation).

Back to the package, as I opened the package I found a type-written letter, now believe this, done on an old type typewriter, probably a Smith Corona, now Google that and see what one looks like. I couldn't tell you how many years since I've seen one of these. I didn't even know you can still get ribbons for them. The letter said, "Conrad, you can read the Sunday comics, look at some beautiful pictures, and make a model. Enjoy."

The box contained a wonderful hardback book called the *B-29 Super Fortress* and a model airplane of the B-29. I put the model together, and it was beautiful and reminded me of old # 214 of which I was the Crew Chief for a long time. As I studied it, it came to me to paint it like our WB-29s in the 58th WRS. I went to a hobby store and spent about $20 on some red, black, and silver model airplane paint. WOW!!! Expensive, you bet!!! A one ounce bottle cost over $4 bucks. I also bought some tiny little letter and number decals and went to work. I painted the tail and the wings red like our planes and painted the deicer boots on the leading edges which were to break the ice off when we started freezing up, which was about all the time. Ice can bring down an airplane pretty quick. (groan)

I totally failed at trying to put on the tiny decal numbers. I ruined $5 worth real quick. I gave up on that so what do I do now? Just a few days later Beverly and I were at Bed Bath & Beyond buying some wedding

Grandpa's Stories

gifts when I discovered their wrapping paper exactly the same color of silver as the airplane. I cut enough extra to make sure I could wrap the gifts and have some left to cut into 8x11 sheets. I put one in my printer and typed up the numbers 4-62214 in several different sizes and BINGO!!! One of them fit perfectly. How smart is that? Only one thing was then lacking. The 58th WRS emblem we had on the nose of our planes for nose art. I thought, well I have that on my 58th webpage, so why not copy and paste it and shrink it to size and just glue it on. That worked out swell.

Now I have an exact replica of the aircraft that I crewed in Alaska. And a famous aircraft I might add. Beverly thinks I am a genius and loves this little model. It sets in our bookcase where everyone who comes in can see it.

MY JOB CHAPTER 1

After the Korean War ended and I was discharged from the United States Air Force, I had the privilege of going to work for American Airlines. This was in March of 1956.

American Airlines had moved their Aircraft and Engine Overhaul facilities to Tulsa, Oklahoma from LaGuardia Air Port in New York City. As that move took place, many New Yorkers re-located their families to Tulsa. Also many came from other stations within the American Airlines network. American later began hiring locally and people came from all over the Midwest and even some foreign countries to work here in Tulsa. Most were from here in Oklahoma, Texas, Arkansas, Louisiana, and Kansas. I worked with a couple of guys from Columbia, South America. As they came, there were many different cultures that came together which made for a lot of laughs.

That is what this story is all about. One funny thing that happened. Jerry Rusden, who came from New York City, met a girl here in Tulsa and they decided to get married. Her home town was Butner, Oklahoma. Jerry was given directions on how to get there from Tulsa to go and meet her

Grandpa's Stories

parents. Take Highway 66 to Bristow and go south on Highway 48, turn right onto Highway 56, go about 10 miles and turn right at the cattle guard and you can see the house from there. Jerry drove and drove but could not find the cattle guard. Finally, he drove back to Butner and called to correct his directions. The conversation went something like this: Jerry, "I have driven this highway for twenty miles twice but I have yet to see a cattle guard." Jerry's future father-in-law knowing that Jerry was from New York City said, "Jerry, do you know what a cattle guard is?" Jerry, "Well, I guess it's a mounted rider on a horse with a gun, maybe?" If you do not know what an Oklahoma cattle guard is, well it is a row of two inch pipes, usually old oil field tubing, formed to go across the bar ditches with enough space that if livestock try to cross it they step through and have to turn around. This takes the place of gates.

And there was a Chinese citizen whose name was Dong, also from New York City. Most everyone called him Fong Dong. He was an avid hunter and competitive shooter. After being here a few days he asked some of his fellow workers where a good place would be to hunt squirrels. One of them told Dong to go north about a mile on Mingo to the "y" and go west about two miles to the woods there and they were full of squirrels. The next day Dong left after work to hunt squirrels. After he had shot about four squirrels, the Mohawk Park Police caught him. Mohawk is the Tulsa City Zoo. Everyone got a good laugh over this, even the Mohawk Park Police were amused after they found that Dong had been set up by a bunch of Okies. Dong later opened a sporting goods store on East Admiral, which is still operated by his children at the time of this writing.

Warren Mires told me a story once that happened when he was just a kid. Warren and his kid brother would crawl under the cattle guard to hide and smoke grape vines. Whenever a car would come down the road they would take turns looking to see was coming. You had to turn your head sideways to get it up through the pipes then turn to see who was coming. One day when they heard a car coming it was his brother's turn to look. He tuned his head and stuck his head up through the pipes only to

Grandpa's Stories

realize that he had waited too long. The car was almost upon the cattle guard. When his brother got his head out of the pipes he was bleeding from the mouth. Warren thought the car had run over his head, but it turned out he had forgot to turn his head sideways and when his chin hit the pipes he bit the end of his tongue. Turned out to be their mother and when the Model A Ford hit the cattle guard it bounced right over him. Warren's brother wasn't hurt too bad but they had a lot of explaining to do about what they were doing under the cattle guard. I still see Warren from time to time.

Horseplay was rampant! I remember the old Engine Buildup Shop's break table that the guys made. It was made like a large picnic table with benches built onto it and covered with stainless steel with a wire running to it hooked up to a 2800 aircraft engine magneto. With a spin of the magneto it would send a stout shock to any one touching the table. Boy, you talk about getting a jump start, there was never a dull moment around that shop.

One day in the Cylinder Shop, Earl Ridenhour and Ronnie Jones were having a major water fight that got a little out of hand. Earl thought he spotted Ronnie with his back turned and talking to the valve grinder operator. He got his gallon bucket of ice cold water out of the deep freeze and crawled on his hands and knees for about fifty feet behind the cylinder track to get into perfect position, then he jumped up and let him have it right in the back. The poor guy screamed, then seemed to be paralyzed for a minute or so. It turned out not to be Ronnie at all, but one of our engineers who was in the shop trying to solve a small problem we had been having with valves.

Some body was always plugging the water fountain, so when you stepped on the pedal it would squirt you right in the shirt pocket. Once while I was running the valve grinders, Elmer Doughty, who was superintendent of Power Plant Overhaul at the time, came down the aisle greeting some of the fellows he knew. He looked over my way and said, "How are you doing today, Layton?" and spun around to get him a cool drink of water. You guessed it, he got it right in the pocket of his clean white starched shirt, which immediately started turning a bright orange color from something he had in his pocket. He turned around and looked at me and said, "Layton! You're the only guy around here who isn't laughing. I know you wouldn't do anything like this, but I bet you know who did." I told him that I didn't have a thing to do with it or any idea who did it. Elmer started laughing and we all had a good laugh. Elmer was a great guy and one of the most respected men who ever worked for AA. He had worked his way up from being a Jr. Mechanic. Some of his ideas are still being practiced today; they are called Elmer checks.

Another day in the Cylinder Shop, Jim Abbott and Les Walters were having a "can you top this" day. When it came time for lunch Les ran by his work station to get his lunch pail. He tore the handle plum off it. Jim had nailed it down to his wooden toolbox. Knowing that it was Abbott's doing, Les went to the coat rack where Abbott had his cute little hat that he always wore and preceded to nail it down to the coat rack. Les had put four nails in the brim and was in the process of bending the nails over on the bottom of the shelf when Raymond Bray walked up. Now Bray was a guy who never messed around with anyone's property and didn't believe in any kind of horseplay on the job. He said, "Les, what are you doing to my hat?" Les spun around and about that time here came Abbott down the aisle wearing his cute little hat which was exactly like Raymond Bray's hat. Raymond was fuming, and Les bought him a new hat.

Les bought him a new Ford pickup truck, bright red. Boy, it was a pretty thing. Almost every day for about a month, someone, usually Lloyd Watkins, would stop along the road somewhere and pick up get an old sofa or mattress or a big overstuffed chair that someone had discarded along Highway 75 and put it in the bed of Les's truck and put a FOR SALE sign on it. After work Les would come out and find a bunch of guys looking to see what he was selling that day. Les would get mad and push it out on the parking lot and drive home madder that an old wet hen.

Grandpa's Stories

Ed "Cannonball" Sturderfelt was the first one at American to buy a Volkswagen when they first came to Tulsa. From day one we started putting a quart of gas in Ed's gas tank every day. After about a month we asked Ed what kind of gas mileage he was getting. Cannonball said, "Look guy's, if I told you guys how good it was doing, you would probably call me a liar." Then we started siphoning out a quart every day for a month. Cannonball had that Volkswagen back to Brown's Auto where he had purchased it three times in one month. When we asked him about his gas mileage again he said, "I don't even want to talk about it." When we told him what we had done he had a good laugh with us. Ed was also from NYC.

There was a fellow names B. B. Gaines who wore his blue jeans rolled up above his ankles. When the Ford Falcons first came out B. B. was the first one at American Airlines to buy one. All the billboards advertised 35 mph, but his would only get about 25 mph. We would kid him about it and he would keep taking it back to Fred Jones Ford to get it checked out. Finally, the service manager told B. B. that if he wanted 35 mph out of his Falcon he would have to do what all the other owners were doing. When B. B. asked him what they were doing, he said lie about it. B. B. would park way out from everyone else so as not to get a scratch on his new car, he was really proud of it. When he would park, he would stop about every twenty feet and turn to look at his car. Someone from time to time would pour some used oil underneath the engine and B. B. would crawl under to see where it was coming from. One day someone put one of those bullet hole decals on his windshield. Bud Shipman I think. When B. B. got close enough to see it really got upset about it; he thought someone had shot his car.

Grandpa's Stories

There were lots of nicknames hung on some of the guys. Someone started calling me "Biscuit" because I was always bringing biscuits with butter and jelly in my lunch. We had Whammy, Downhill, Tripod, Wormy, Barrel Head, Ironhead, Jughead, K-Mart Lilly, Lucy, Augie, Heavy,

Moose, Peanuts, Gundy, and Bones to name a few. Lots of different parts would get renamed after someone screwed one up like Joe Boxes, Mazie Rings, Gundy tubes, etc.

Many, many years ago a bunch of guys went to California on a field trip. One of the guys bought a crate of fresh oranges. One of the guys, Carl Guthery, thought it would be nice to spike them up a little. He bought a bottle of vodka and some syringes and gave every one of them a shot. Captain Jack Lee thought they were the best oranges he had ever tasted, and ate way too many, you can guess the rest. I still laugh when I think of Bill McKinny's Joe Palooka's Humphrey Mobile. (You might want to Google that.) I could go on and on and never run out of funnies that would bring a laugh or smile to someone, but to really sum up American Airlines would be to say it was 37 of the best years of my life, a great place to work. We had the best mechanics, the best supervisors—well, some were good. I worked for the best one, Jim Kelly. No other airline or factory could overhaul and build a better aircraft engine than American Airlines. I can recall representatives from all over the world coming to Tulsa Overhaul Base to see how we were overhauling aircraft and engines. Our

Engineering Department had our specifications closer than any factory specs.

I'm going to close this story on one last funny note. After I became an inspector and was in Central Inspection or Quality Assurance as it was called for a time, we all chipped in on money to buy a remote car about 12 inches long. We took Styrofoam and made a body to look like a huge rat, tail and all. It even had whiskers. Some times when things got really dull we would get him out and let him play in the aisle. We had on occasion been threatened with termination if we didn't quit scaring people with our harmless little pet.

When Vice President George Herbert Walker Bush was running for president, his entourage flew into Tulsa for a brief time and was going to come through the plant to greet us and try to muster some votes. We thought this would be a good time to exercise our cute little pet. When our supervisor got wind of what was going to happen, he got very upset. He threatened to fire every last one of us if we even attempted to open the cabinet where the rat slept in his off time. Needless to say we thought it best to leave him there. This story was written January 15, 2000. With more to come later.

MY JOB CHAPTER 2

I ended Chapter 1 on a serious note, now I want to get back to some very good stuff.

We had a supervisor in Central Inspection with the initials J. W. R. who took things a little too seriously at times. Once while Claude Bernard and I were out for our noon walk, we entered the shop from the back door and every one was ganged up around J. W. R.'s desk. When J. W. spotted us coming he summoned us up to the desk also. We walked up and Claude said, "What's going on?" J. W. pointed over to his little Igloo ice chest which he used for a lunch pail. All you could see was the very top of his ice tea jar lid. The ice chest had been filled with some kind of spray foam which had set up as solid as a rock. It looked like it had been either Niedercorned or Henched. Frank Niedercorn and Dave Henche were two guys in our crew. I began to laugh. J. W. said, "Layton, this is not all that very funny." J. W. told us that the ice chest had been given to him by Dolly Parton, the female country singer, while he was working as an engineer on the building of Opryland in Nashville, Tennessee. He said the ice chest had great sentimental value to him, and added that he was going to find out who had done this and see that they were punished. J. W. and I got along very well together and he later came back to my bench and asked if I knew who had done this dreadful deed. I told him that I had no idea who had done this and wouldn't tell him if I did. I said, "J. W., the smartest thing you could do is forget it, let it pass and try to act like it never happened. If Dolly is really a friend, call her and she will probably send you a new ice chest." I told him that some guys in the shop would really make life miserable for him if they thought they could get under his skin.

We had another Inspection Supervisor just down the hall who was over the turbine blade section of Inspection. He was a young guy who had once worked in the Wheel & Brake Shop as a mechanic until he really messed up some work in there. I don't remember all the particulars, but the company had to take the tools out of his hands. (grin) That is when the company made him a supervisor. He had never worked as an Inspector. He always came down to our shop for coffee. On this occasion someone had drawn up a cartoon of a mechanic really messing up a brake job and had enough copies made to post on all the bulletin boards at American Airlines. We had a lot of really good cartoonists working there. Anyway young Rotrammel came to get some coffee, and was really mad. He said he was going to fire that #%&*%^^$^&&^%& Bill Shawn, who he was blaming for the cartoons. I told young Rotrammel to just cool off and laugh with them and forget it. I told Rotrammel that Bill Shawn had seen a hundred like him come and go, but he was still here. He didn't listen to me, he raised cane about the matter, and a couple of weeks later the company sent him to Denver to work as a ticket clerk.

Grandpa's Stories

One day in Central Inspection, Claude Bernard and I decided to start walking at noon. We both bought some good walking shoes. One day while we were out walking, "Sugarless," short for Max Palmer, came over to our bench and saw our shoes setting there empty beside our chairs. He started looking around to see if any other shoes were setting around. He summoned a few of the other guys to look things over. A couple of them thought the Rapture had come and they had been left behind. About that time, we came back. They said, "Boy, are we glad to see you guys!"

I was setting at my bench carving a carousel horse one day when I sensed someone standing behind me. I turned around and there stood John Ebberstein. John was at that time the Director of JT-8 Engine Overhaul. He had once been my Supervisor in Central Inspection. He said, "What are you doing C. R.?" I said, "Hello John, I'm just relieving a little stress." John said, "You mean that will relieve stress." I said, "Sure John, if you would like, I'll give you some carving lessons." He said, "I may take you up on that" and turned and walked away. Later John came back into our shop and told me what he really came down for was to ask me if I would take a company position as an analyst (this was a job that analyzed what was wrong with parts or what caused crashes, but I wanted hands on work). I told him flat out no! He said would you be willing to go on a special assignment for about six months or a year. I told him I might do that, what did he have in mind? He wanted me to review all the engine parts that went through NDT or Non Destructive Testing. This shop was working two twelve hour shifts seven days a week and John wanted to know if there was any way to cut down on this. Some of the Inspectors in NDT were making over $150,000 a year. That compared to his $80,000. I took this assignment, and that could be a whole complete story on its own.

About six months before I retired my Central Inspection Supervisor was sent to Tokyo, Japan to set up a terminal and maintenance program for a new travel route with American Airlines to Japan. I was approached and asked to take his place as Supervisor while he was gone. Estimated to be a month. I accepted the temporary job. I was over three of our shops. Central

Inspection, Non-destructive Testing (NDT), and the Engine Cleaning Shop. It was bit of a task to say the least. After about two weeks I went to Charlie, our Director, and told him it was no wonder he was having trouble keeping Supervisors, he was killing them with overload. I knew of no other Supervisor in Power Plant Overhaul that had more than one shop to run. He didn't like what I was saying at all. He just said, "Well, Jim will be back from Japan in a couple of weeks to relieve you." It turned out Jim was gone almost four months. I'm thinking that was one of the reasons why I chose to retire so early at age 57. Charlie was fired by AA shortly after I retired. Sorry Charlie.

In the 37 years I worked for American Airlines, there were thousands of events that I wish I had written down. Occasionally I can remember one of them, so who knows how long this story will end up being.

January 2003

BASS FISHING

I have always loved fishing, no matter what type fish we were going for. Sometimes catfish, crappie, perch, or bass, it didn't matter, it was fun to catch any fish. From the early days of my youth, I remember fishing. I've fished with a whole lot of different guys but my favorite fishing partner was my lovely wife Beverly. I have fished ponds, creeks, rivers, and lakes, it doesn't matter to me if I'm catching fish. Our all-time favorite fish to eat is crappie. Probably next would be largemouth bass, but I can eat most any of them.

Back in the late 1950s I really got into bass fishing. Lake Tenkiller here in Oklahoma was at the time rated the #1 bass fishing lake in the USA. Only about an hour's drive from Tulsa, it was easy to get to. On a whole lot of Fridays, I would leave work and come home to load my boat and head for Lake Tenkiller to fish the night away. I would usually fish until about 9-10 on Saturday morning then head for home. Nearly always with a good

Grandpa's Stories

string of bass. Another lake I liked to fish was Eucha which was even closer than Tenkiller.

Many of the guys I worked with at American Airlines were fishing Lake Bull Shoals in Arkansas which boasted many big bass being caught. One of my really good friends and quail hunting buddies was always trying to get me to go to Bull Shoals with him for the weekend. I didn't really like spending the weekend away from my wife and my kids so I always turned him down. One weekend in April he ask me again and said his family was going with him and I could take my family also. I agreed and my whole family was really looking forward to the weekend getaway. Finally Friday came and we left from work and headed for Harrison, Arkansas.

We arrived at our destination about 6 p.m. and unloaded. We were all staying in two cabins that we had reserved. After getting the families settled in, Marv and I went down to boat dock where we had a 16 foot cedar striped boat reserved. These boats were made to be guide boats and they were great for two guys to fish out of. We mounted Marvin's 18 horst Evinrude motor on it, loaded our gear, and went back up to the camp to eat supper.

Just before dark we were on the lake fishing. I knew absolutely nothing about Bull Shoals but Marv had lots of experience on the lake. Back in those days I made all my own tackle, jigs, spinner baits, etc. If my memory serves me correctly, I rigged up one of my handmade black jigs with a 10 inch eel, also made by myself and Marv hooked up a single spin with a Uncle Josh's frog chunk. We were strictly after lunkers. (My four grandsons now have the left overs of that tackle.) It hadn't been 10 minutes until I caught the first bass, a large mouth about 3 pounds. I started to dig out my stringer, but Marv said, "What are you doing? Don't string up that little thing, let him grow up some. We don't string anything under 4 pounds." So I groaned a little and tossed him back in.

Grandpa's Stories

Me with Marv and Big Bass at Bull Shoals

I caught 3 bass in a row, stringing only one that was 5 1/2 lbs. That was when Marv changed over to a black jig & eel. At exactly midnight I hooked a good one, it turned out to be the largest fish caught there over the entire week. It was an 8 pounds, 14 ounce largemouth. Marv said if that fish had been a female carrying eggs it would have been a 10 pounder. Bull Shoals was part of the White River Playground Association and awarded the fisherman that caught the largest bass of the week with a certificate and a gold pin of a jumping bass with the weight written on it. Really nice little gift if you are in to that type of thing, I liked it. Marv said it was beginner's luck.

Marv and I wound up the night with 16 fish over 4lbs, just four below the limit which was 10 per day per person. We didn't see another boat that came in with anything like that. I put the big one on ice because I was going to have it mounted when I got home. It hangs on my den wall now.

Melody with Crappie

Later in the day, Joyce, Marv's wife, agreed to watch Tommy for a while so I could take Beverly and Melody out in the boat for a little while. I had bought Melody a little Zebco fishing rod and I tied on a small doll fly. We were anchored in a small cove and she was fishing. Beverly and I were sitting there talking and I heard Melody grunting, I looked over and her rod was bent down under the boat and about to break. She was trying to reel it in but was struggling. I told her to just stay with it and keep reeling. When I saw the fish she had on I was really surprised, it was about the biggest crappie I had ever seen. We got it in the boat and I strung it up. When we got back to the dock the owner was there doing some work. He saw the crappie and wanted to weigh it. I told him my daughter caught it. He couldn't believe it. A couple of guys came in about that time and saw the crappie. One said, "Man, you caught

Grandpa's Stories

a dandy there, I've been fishing all my life and I've never caught one that big." I said, "I didn't catch it. My daughter did." He looked at Melody like he didn't believe me and I told him that was her first fish. She wasn't 3 years old yet. It weighed 1-3/4 lbs, a very nice crappie by any standard. After all these years of fishing I've caught about 10 or 12 that size or bigger, 2/14 has been the largest.

Bull Shoals Fisherman of the Week

The next night I also caught the biggest one, it weighed 7/10. We ate a lot of fish sticks for the next couple of weeks. I wound up going to Bull Shoals about three more times and all four times I was the fisherman of the week. After that fourth time Marv never ask me to go again. (groan) Oh well, I still had Eucha and Tenkiller. Was I a better bass fisherman than Marv? No way! Marv could think like a bass and decide where in a hurry where we should be fishing. He could get right on top of them. Marv and another friend that haunted Bull Shoals were approached by Challenger Boat Co. and asked to design what they thought would be the perfect boat to bass fish out of. They both incorporated their ideas, like a flat deck to stand on, trolling motor, live well, good seats for two fishermen, and a place to store equipment. Challenger then came out with what we now know as a bass boat, and every boat company in the country has copied it. Marv and Burl both were given one of the first boats to come out of their factory.

I had lots of fishing buddies, I fished more with Chuck Rogers than anyone else. Chuck was a great companion. My next door neighbor back then was Delbert Rahe, a teacher at our school. He would come over once in a while and ask me to go fishing with him. Tommy liked to go with us. We liked going to Shell Creek, a small lake just west of Sand Springs. We also liked to fish ponds. Once he wanted to take me to Crescent, OK where his old family home had once been, a brother now owned it. There were five ponds on the property, All the way down there he told me about "Big Boy," a huge largemouth bass that had been hooked by everybody in the family

Grandpa's Stories

but had just broken their line. I told him that they just weren't rigged up to catch big bass like that, Delbert said, "I hope you hook into "Big Boy," you'll lose him too." Well, guess what? I did get hooked up with him and got him into the boat. I told Delbert that I was going to release it and he didn't want me to. He said the pond would be better off with him out of it. "Big Boy" wasn't the heaviest bass I ever caught but was certainly the longest one. It measured 27 ½ inches and weighed 7/12. If "Big Boy" had been a big lake bass he would have been 10 or more pounds.

I always loved fishing with my son Tom. By the time he grew old enough, Keystone had been built and had filled up and turned out to be a wonderful lake. I did lots of fishing there because it was so close. I soon discovered House Creek on Keystone which became my favorite fishing spot. When I went to House Creek I would fish some for bass and some for crappie. It was really a hot spot. Tom was also a pretty good fisherman. I recall we almost froze to death once while fishing Keystone. It came up a sudden thunderstorm and we pulled the boat up on a bank and got under some trees. We got soaked to the bone. It was so cold that we were hugging each other trying to stay warm. When I got home I went to a store and bought two ponchos which I still have and never worn.

Fort Gibson Lake was always good to me. I remember once Beverly and I were trolling down in the Snug Harbor area when she hooked a good one. It had made a couple of good jumps and I knew it was at least a 5 pounder. About that time a guy came flying out of the harbor in a big cabin cruiser and deliberately cut her line. I could have shot him.

Pretty Water was also one of my favorite places to fish. I could come home from work and load up and be there in 30 minutes. Biggest fish I ever caught there was a 6 ½ pounder but I lost count of the 5 pounders I pulled out of there.

This story may sound like I'm really being braggadocious, but I once heard Dizzy Dean that called the Baseball Game of the Week with Peewee Reese, both Hall of Famers, say that <u>if you've done it, it ain't bragging.</u>

Grandpa's Stories

If you have never fished, you have really cheated yourself. Get out and fish.

THE BEST CHRISTMAS GIFT

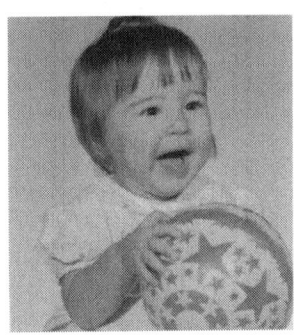
Melody

My wife Beverly and I were married January 11, 1957. I was working for American Airlines and she was working at Tri-State Insurance. Along about the summer of that year she began to have morning sickness. Well, you know what that usually means. Beverly was pregnant with our first child. We had just bought a lot to build our new house. We had just also purchased us a new Fairlane 500 Ford two-door hardtop automobile, willow green and white. It was the prettiest car in Tulsa.

About a month later, Beverly began to have problems carrying the baby. Her doctor advised her to quit her job and not to do any ironing, sweeping, or climbing stairs if she expected to have this baby. That wasn't very good news for either of us. We were living in an upstairs apartment, located on the corner of 7th and Lansing and we both loved that little apartment, but we would have done anything to keep from losing our baby. We rented a small house on the west side of Tulsa so Beverly wouldn't have any stairs to climb, and I managed to work enough overtime to keep our car payments paid on time.

As Christmas drew near we were going to have Christmas dinner with my family and Beverly's mother and Uncle John. Beverly was supposed to make one of her famous "Chocolate Mayonnaise Cakes." Christmas morning about four o'clock in the morning she woke me up to tell me it was time. Of course I was very calm. I scurried about trying to gather everything we would need, and headed for St. Johns Hospital. At five something that morning Beverly gave me the best Christmas I have ever received. Her name was Melody Joy Layton, she weighed 6 lbs. and 11ozs. As we celebrate Christmas this year, the year 2000, Melody will be forty-three years old and has blessed us with another son, Mike her husband, and two terrific grandchildren, Maeve and Niall McMahon.

It would be needless to say that we didn't have that famous Chocolate Mayonnaise Cake that day, and my dear mother made reference to that fact for many years, all in joking of course.

December 1, 2000

BUILDING OUR HOUSE

When Beverly and I first married, I was working for American Airlines and her at Tri-State Insurance. We immediately decided to buy us a new car. We decided on the Ford Fairlane 500 Hardtop. It was a beautiful automobile. At the time we were renting a great apartment on the corner of 7th and Lansing in Tulsa. Beverly could walk to work from there. We both loved that apartment but soon decided that a stack of rent receipts were not worth much.

Then we decided we needed to own a house and not rent. We began looking for property to build on and found this lot where we now live. We had looked everywhere for the ideal place for us, Owasso, Sand Springs, Bruner Hill, and all over Tulsa, and our Pastor (Gene Winfrey) found out we were looking for a place to build a home and told about the lot next to his house in Berryhill. We went over to Berryhill to view the property. It was the adjoining acre to his and Wanna's lot. It was his horse pasture. Gene had quit the rodeo and had sold his horse. Gene had been the highest ranking Trick Rider in the USA when he decided to quit. The neighborhood was called Pleasure Acres and there were very few homes already built in this addition. We began driving around Berryhill to get an idea of what we were getting into. When we drove by Berryhill School we were sold on Berryhill. It was beautiful little campus and the football field and everything had just been mowed and someone was touching up

Grandpa's Stories

paint on the stadium. We agreed that this was the school that we wanted our children to attend.

Gene made us a price we could not turn down of $1350.00. I went to our credit union at AA and applied for a loan for that amount. No problems--the next day I picked up the check. We made the deal with Gene and Wanna and were so happy to now be property owners for the first time. Well, almost the first, I already owned one square inch of land at North Pole, Alaska which I had purchased while stationed in Fairbanks. Before we ever started building we were offered more than double what we had paid for the lot.

Almost every day we would drive over to Berryhill just to see if our lot was still there, it never moved one time before we finally built on it. I really had to be careful when I mowed the acre, there were about three families of Horn Frogs living there and I didn't want to bother them. Shortly after buying our lot Beverly became pregnant with our daughter Melody Joy. So we decided to wait awhile to build. Lo and behold, Beverly started having complications with carrying our baby and had to quit her job at Tri-State. That left us with only my income. We postponed building but decided to go ahead and have plans drawn up for our dream home. We put all our ideas together on what we really wanted our home to look like and how big, etc. and I took them to an architect. He drew up our plans and blueprints for $75.00. We almost wore out the plans just looking at them before we ever started building. We talked to a good friend of ours who was a builder, Howard Gwartney, about building our home. He agreed to have his crew do all the rough in work for us and we would do the finishing up. While we were waiting for the opportunity to start our project (Short of MONEY) Howard came to up and asked if he could use our plans to build a house on another property and we agreed to allow him to do that.

While we were waiting we would still go and check on our lot in Berryhill. Howard started building a house straight across the street from our lot. It appeared it was going to be a large nice place. As it developed I went over to Howard one afternoon after I got home from work and there laid out were the plans for our home. I asked Howard what was going on. He told me this was the house I asked if I could use your plan for. I about blew my stack right there. I said, "Howard, why didn't you mention that you wanted to build it across from our house." He started hem hawing around about how sorry he was. Well when we finally were ready to build we altered the plans so it wouldn't look exactly like the house across the street. I would like to have shot Howard at that time. I altered the front porch and took 5 feet off of the living and dining room. I'm sorry now that I changed anything.

When Howard turned it over to me to finish I remember a lot of friends that came over to help do one thing or another. My brother-in-law at that time Les Littlefield was a big help. One of my best friends Bill Sasser had painting experience and he helped a lot with that. Orval Bryant, a fishing buddy and old friend of my Mom and Pop, taught me how to lay the rock. That was about the hardest job of all. It was very slow.

Later we added on a 26x18 foot addition to our den and a wood burning fireplace. This was one of the smartest things I ever did. The whole family has had a lot of enjoyment in that den. My son Tom had a big part in helping me add this room, I could not have done it without him. Beverly and I completely designed it. We put in everything that we thought we wanted. Fireplace, the five mullion bow window, French door, etc. Today as I write this story we still love our den and neither of us want to change anything.

I remember when I started looking for rock to match what we had put on the front of our house. I soon discovered it was no longer available. The Arkansas stone quarries had priced themselves out of the market. When I

Grandpa's Stories

bought the original rock it was $11 a ton. Fourteen years later it was $44 a ton if you could find it. I would be needing a lot of tons of rock and ledge stone because I had decided to put it all around the house and build our rock planters. So what did I do? I started looking at rock and dirt fills or dumps where someone might have dumped some old stone like mine. I was able to find quite a bit of which I would load in my pickup and bring home. A little later the Broken Arrow Expressway was started up and a lot of demolition was going on. I drove everywhere I knew it was going to be to see if any buildings or homes had the rock I wanted. That became a life saver. There was an insurance company on 15th and Cincinnati coming down. I stopped and asked if I could buy the rock on it. I was told if I was willing to unstack it and haul it off I could have it. I stopped there every day for about a week taking that rock. The same happened on 11th and Main. There was restaurant coming down and they gave me the same deal. Then Beverly and I found a city building just off Denver and 14th that had large planters in from with tons of rock and the same ledge stone that would match our house. I asked Beverly to check on it with the City of Tulsa the next day. They told her that it would be up for auction and what day. On that day she got there early and asked the guy in charge how she could bid on that rock. He told her to just stand over there and he would get the sale started with the planters before they went inside. He told when he opened the bid to say I'll give a dollar. She did and he immediately said sold to the little lady for $1. She was so excited that she called me at work to tell me she got it for a dollar. That was all the rock I need to finish the job. All of the rock I found was not Arkansas Stone but rather Colorado Stone some with a pinkish tint but I was able to blend it in with the other.

    The front porch and den I added on has increased the value of our house at least $ 50,000. I need to pat myself on the back for a job well done. And Mom too. Also my children for the sacrifices they had to make while we were doing all that. Thanks Beverly and Melody and Tom.

July 2016

Grandpa's Stories

LAYTON CAMPING TRIPS

When I was very little I more or less grew up camping out. Sometimes very crude and not really planned to say the least.

Tommy and Melody

After Beverly and I had married and had our children we decided to teach them to camp out. We began to set up to camp out. At first we had a couple of trips to Arkansas to Nimrod Dam on Memorial Day weekends, we really liked the long weekends. We would camp just below the dam on the Fourche La Fave River. This was before we got the tent and the kids would sleep in the back of our Rambler station wagon and me and Mom on the ground nearby. On these trips there were three families of us, the Rogers' clan and the Mosses. By the time we all got situated there below the dam it would look like a band of Gypsies had come along. Chuck and Jean Marie Rogers had 5 children and Chuck's Dad Freeman always came along. Johnny and Betty Moss's 2 and our 2. That made a total of 16 people. We would always have a big fish fry on Sunday afternoon and pack up on Monday and come home. I remember a bunch of Chuck's kinfolks from Russellville and Goose Camp, Arkansas would come down on Sunday for the fish fry. They were some pretty colorful folks. This really got us to liking camping.

When our children were very young we had an opportunity to buy a very nice camping tent from our neighbors across the street, the Mouser's, Felix and Okla. It was a 10x12 foot tent with flaps that would let down over the screens in case of rain or cold. It also had a good floor. We went out and bought 4 folding cots and some more essentials needed for camping. I already had a good Coleman camping stove and lantern and plenty of good flashlights. One of our earliest trips was to "Dog Patch" in Harrison, Arkansas. This was a little campground on a beautiful little creek based on the comic strip Lil' Abner. The kids had a ball there. I remember Melody and Tommy, along with a couple of other kids, making a crude little raft

Grandpa's Stories

and floating around the creek on it. Tommy learned really quickly that every camp site had food. He would go from tent to tent to see and sample what they were having for dinner.

Fiddler's Bend was one of our favorite places to pitch our tent. Fiddler's Bend was a great campground right on the Illinois River where Flint Creek dumped into it. You could swim in either the ice cold creek or the much warmer river. We did both. You could put a watermelon in the creek and it would get plenty cold. Nobody would ever bother it.

The first time we went to Fiddler's Bend we stayed in a one room cabin right on the creek. This was the 4th of July weekend and it was hot. We would always leave as early on Friday evening as we could so we could get a good camping site. We took only sheets and pillows to make our beds. I remember the cabins were $4 a night. They weren't anything fancy, just four bare wooden walls with a floor and roof over it. Two beds and a table and four chairs. It was great until the sun went down, then it started getting cold. I remember Mom trying to cover up the kids with anything she could find that was dry. We were up really early that next morning. Once our next door neighbors went to Fiddler's Bend with us, Billy and Delbert and their daughter Kay Rahe. It was another long weekend and the weather was great. We had a great time with them. Our kids loved them and we considered them best friends. Without Billy knowing it Beverly took a snapshot of her just as she was stepping out of the outhouse. We still have that photo.

Tommy and I got to the point where we could put the tent up and set up our cots long before Mom could get supper ready. All the family had a job to do in setting up. Melody would fetch water from the pump and help Mom get supper on the table. She also was the one who would make our beds for us. She loved to read and always took some books to read when things got boring. (grin)

We went to Keystone Lake a time or two. I would also take our 12-foot Jon (flat-bottom fishing boat) boat and motor and we would fish and swim.

Grandpa's Stories

On another 4th of July weekend we went to Lake Eucha Park about 60 miles east of Tulsa. Some of our friends Bill and Rita Cunningham and their two daughters were going to come on Saturday evening to meet us and camp for the night.

We set up camp, had supper, and I took the kids out fishing for a while. Just before dark we came back and got ready for bed. Do you remember how cold I said we got that weekend long ago at Fiddler's Bend about freezing to death? Well, you would think we would have learned a lesson, right?!! Well, before morning arrived we were all in the same boat, covering up with anything we could find. Saturday morning when we got through eating breakfast I told Beverly to go into the little town of String about 10 miles down the road and buy some blankets. She was only able to find two blankets for sale. I told her to go the campground office and call Rita and tell her to go by our house and take all the quilts and blankets off our bed and bring them with them when they came. Bill and Rita owned the Berryhill Grocery Store. They had a big camper on Bill's pickup truck. Saturday night we stayed really warm for a change. I soon learned that anytime you're around cold water after the sun goes down, it can get pretty cool at night.

I wouldn't exactly call this camping but there were many times that Chuck Rogers and I would go somewhere and fish all night. Places like Greenleaf Lake or Low Water Dam on Grand River. We would plan for Beverly and Jean Marie to bring the kids the next morning and cook breakfast on the banks of whatever we fished that particular night. They would go by somewhere and get a couple of pounds of bacon and a couple dozen eggs and bread and coffee and we'd have a time to meet them. Jean Marie would always make "creek bank" coffee. I remember Beverly couldn't stand to drink it, but the rest of us thought it was great. Beverly would close her eyes and drink it anyway. You make it with water right out of the river or lake and just pour in the coffee and boil it really good. Then you let the grounds settle to the bottom and it was ready to pour. Good stuff. Boy, would it be fun to go back and do it all over. 2016

Grandpa's Stories

OUR FAMILY VACATION TO THE CLINCH MOUNTAINS

Aunt Ida

The year was 1963. We had bought a new 1962 Rambler Classic station wagon the previous year. In 1960 Beverly's mother Martha had a brain tumor and had to have surgery. The surgery left Martha partially paralyzed and Martha's cousin who we called Aunt Ida came to Tulsa from Kingsport, Tennessee to help care for her. Beverly and I and both of the kids just loved Aunt Ida. She told us all about the Clinch Mountains where she and Martha had grown up and all about the cousins and such that were still in Kingsport, Tennessee and Virginia. Ida wanted us to come visit her as soon as we could.

We made our big plans for the fall of 1963 to go to Tennessee and Virginia and circle down through Georgia, Alabama, and Louisiana. We loaded the Rambler and on Friday after the Berryhill High School Football Game we headed east up I-44 through St. Louis, Missouri, and down through Cairo, Illinois and into Kentucky where we had to cross the Cumberland River on a ferry boat. The ferry was a first for our family. We then entered Tennessee and went to Nashville. We arrived there about 8:00 a.m. in the morning and located a very nice motel not far from "The Grand Ole Opry" which we would be going to that Saturday night. The Opry was great; we had lots of fun. After leaving Nashville we went to see the Hermitage, the home and farm of Andrew Jackson. Leaving there we saw a car in the parking lot with a Berryhill Chief tag on the front of it. We never did find out who else was there from Berryhill.

Late the next evening we were entering Kingsport. Ida had told us to stop somewhere and call because we would never be able to find their place. I pulled into a Kayo Service Station there on the main drag to make the call. As I walked in there were two guys talking. I asked if I could use the phone. One of them pointed to the pay phone over on the wall. I was dialing Ida's number when I heard one of the guys say, "Yahh, one of them was sitting at the desk and the other was standing over there, neither one knew what hit them." I started looking around then to see what was going on. I could see blood everywhere behind the desk. I asked the one talking what had happened there. When he turned around I could see his badge and knew he was some kind of law enforcement officer. He said, "We had a double murder here about an hour ago." About that time Ida picked up the phone. When I told her where we were, she said, "Stay right there, and Ray will be down there in about ten minutes." I said, "We won't be here. We will be two blocks down the street. Tell Ray to look for our Red Rambler. They just had some serious trouble here." Ray Dean was Ida's son-in-law, married to her daughter Eula.

Their home was right on the Tennessee and Virginia state line. When we got there, I asked Ida where her son was. She said he was in the hospital recovering from stab wounds he had received up at one of the dives on the state line. We never got to see him.

The next day we started the trek into the Clinch Mountains. The Clinch Mountains were settled by veterans of the Revolutionary War that were given land grants for their service to the State of Virginia. They were very hardy people. Ida told us that no matter where we were, if someone offered us something, not to refuse it. If we didn't want it we could dump it somewhere. It was their custom to give visitors something to take home.

First we went to the south slope of what they called the "Big Ridge" and "Big Poor Boy Valley." We saw the grave yard where Beverly's grandparents were buried, and went on to Possum Creek to see George and Rudolf Calhoun, first cousins of Beverly's mother Martha. Upon arriving there we were told by one of the women that George and Rudolf were over on Camel Back Ridge cutting and staking tobacco. We left Melody and Tommy there to play with their kids, (lots of them) and took off across the country--Ida knew exactly where that ridge was. First we came upon George and Aunt Ida introduced us to him. George put his hands to his

Grandpa's Stories

Shelton/Calhouns—Rudolf is Baby on the right.

mouth as to make a bull horn and yelled down the ridge to Rudolf saying, "Rudolf, come on up here, we've got kin folk come all the way from Oklahomy." Rudolf yelled back, "George, ask that feller how many chillen he's got." George looked at me and said, "How many chillen you got?" I told him two, a boy and a girl. George cupped his hands again, "Rudolf, this feller says he got two." Rudolf calls back and says, "George, iffin that feller ain't got no more than two chillen, he ain't worth lookin at, I ain't commin up there." George was really embarrassed. He looked at me and said, "Don't pay no mind to that brother of mine. He looks down on me cause I only got twelve chillens." I said, "How many does Rudolf have?" He said, "Fourteen now and one on the way." We met another cousin who owned the General Store there in the valley. I can't recall his name but I remember he wanted me to see his corn patch out back on the hill side. He said it would make at least two gallons (White Lightnin') to the acre.

Aunt Lizzie

We went to see Aunt Lizzie and had lunch there. Lizzie was Martha's aunt and was ninety-three at that time. She still cut and staked her own tobacco, and could still hang it in her three story "bakker barn." She was the wife of a Baptist minister and the church was on her property. Lizzie couldn't read but she wanted us to see her church and where her pew was. Every Sunday she would quote a scripture from the Bible. As we ate lunch there were two teenage girls that stood by the table waving "flybushes." The food was excellent. Flybushes were rolled up newspapers with about ten inches on the ends shredded to shoo the flies away from the food.

Later that evening while having supper with cousin Frank and Alice Catron, a young man knocked on the kitchen door. Alice allowed him to enter and told him that Rose, their teenage daughter, was in the living room. He leaned his rifle in the corner of the room, took his gun belt off, rolled it up and laid it on the cabinet close to the door and went to the living room. I asked Frank if he was a lawman or something. Frank said, "No, he is just from another valley and the last time he came calling on our daughter, someone slashed the tires on his 57 Chevy. Here when you go out of your own valley looking for a woman you are looking for trouble." (They had screens on the windows and flybushes were not necessary.)

Frank was a lineman for an electric company and had a lot of empty wire spools which he made beautiful tables out of. I commented on how nice they were and he wanted to give me some to bring home with me. It was pretty obvious that we didn't have room for them in our car. Instead they gave us some canned goods that they had just canned at the community cannery. We were glad to accept these although nothing was labeled. Alice knew exactly what they were by the way they were placed in the cellar.

Near their home was a long railroad tunnel through the mountain. The next morning, we took our kids and two of the Catron children and went to explore the tunnel. Frank had said that only one train a day came through there and it was in the afternoon. We were about one hundred yards into the tunnel when we heard a train whistle. I told all the kids to run for it and we started back the way we had come. There were my two kids, age 5 and 3, and Frank's two youngest kids. We barely made it out of the tunnel and I threw kids up on the embankment to get them clear of the tracks. Beverly and I had to hug the embankment to keep from being hit by the train. It was really a close call and I have had no desire to enter any more tunnels.

Grandpa's Stories

When we left the mountains and Kingsport, we headed south and through the Smoky Mountains and on down to Atlanta, Georgia to see old friends, Gene and Wanna Winfrey who were pastoring a church there, then on to Stone Mountain to see Talbert Moore and his family (Talbert was a Baptist preacher who came up here to preach a revival for Gene). Talbert and I went bass fishing while we were there. We then went to Gadsden, Alabama to see T.D. and Joy Burgess. (T.D. was the assistant pastor to Gene Winfrey at Crusader's). While we were in Gadsden there was a church bombing in Birmingham, Alabama that made the national news. Someone had thrown a bomb through a basement window into a Sunday School room and it killed four young black girls. The next evening when we left Gadsden to go to New Orleans, we were entering Birmingham and the street we were on was lined with black people, there were several houses on fire and burning down. I looked at the gas gauge and it was on empty. Just as soon as we were past the trouble I saw a service station, wheeled in, and told the kids to stay in the car. I stayed just long enough to put five gallons of gas in and pulled out of there and headed for New Orleans. About a hundred miles from there I stopped to fill our gas tank and discovered that I had left our gas cap back in Birmingham. I let them keep it and bought a new one.

We pulled into New Orleans early the next morning around 7 a.m. and started looking for some place to eat. Everywhere we went was closed. About 9:30 I pulled into a gas station and asked where we could find a place to get some breakfast. The guy said, "Well, sure. Just right on down the street about half a mile there is a big blue stucco building. It's probably the best restaurant in town and they serve a wonderful breakfast." I said, "OK," and we went on down there. But there were only one or two cars in the lot. We walked in and over here on the right was the Blue Room, and over there was the Pink Room and over there was the Coral Room. Anyway, I heard some commotion in one room so we walked over there. This guy came over to us and he had on this tuxedo almost, black tie, white shirt. And he asked, "Can I help you folks?" and I said, "Yeah, we were told there is really a good breakfast here." He said, "Well, who in the world would have told you that?" And I said, "The guy down the street at one of the filling stations." He said, "Good grief, we don't even open up until 11. Well, find a table. Sit down. I guess we can rustle up something. Is ham and eggs ok?" I said, "That sounds really good." He said, "Some coffee and toast?" I said, "Some milk for the kids." So they brought us all a glass of water. And he was doing most of it. He was going back and forth to the kitchen. He came out with a platter with a big pitcher of milk and set it on the table, with glasses for the kids and cups for us. Then he comes out with a pot of coffee. Then here he comes with a big platter of toast, then a platter of eggs. Oh, and he brought four plates. Then he brought a platter with at least three ham steaks. They were probably at least 3/8 inch thick. Well, you know what a ham steak looks like. The kids were going "wow" every time they brought out a new platter. I was kinda in awe myself. Beverly looked at me and I said, "Don't even think about it. Let's just enjoy this breakfast." Anyway, we ate and we ate. I don't think we ate all the ham. In fact, I don't think we even cut one of the ham steaks, I'm not sure. But we had plenty to eat and drink. Then the guy came back over and asked, "Would you like anything else?" And I told him, "No, but I am wondering how much I am going to owe you." He said, "Ah, would about four dollars be ok?" I said, "Oh, that would be wonderful," thinking it was going to be fifteen or twenty dollars. We had a good time in Louisiana and headed home the next day. When we got home, we agreed that we had fun but were ready to be in our own beds once again.

While unloading the next day, Beverly said, "How am I supposed to know what is in these cans?" I told her to only open one can at a meal.

In June of the year 2003, Beverly and I went back to the Clinch Mountains to see Ray and Eula Dean and some of the other relatives that are still living. The Catron girl, Barbara, and older sister Rose came to see us at the Dean's home. Barbara said she remembered me, I saved her life in the train tunnel.

Grandpa's Stories

THE FUN YEARS

The Jest of Peewee Baseball: It all started the summer of 1967. A friend of mine came to me and asked if my son Tommy was going to play Peewee Baseball next year. I said, "Gosh, I don't know, I guess so." He said, "Why don't you take some of these kids that are going into second grade and start practicing them a little, this summer. The competition is so great you need to start them now and teach them some fundamentals."

Our city of Tulsa Kids Baseball Program started for boys in the second grade or eight years of age. Little did I know what I was getting myself into. It lasted eight years.

I put up a sign at the Berryhill Grocery Store asking for boys going into second grade who wanted to play baseball next year to call me. I had about seven or eight boys interested. (Actually their parents were interested.) One boy showed up wearing a right handed ball glove; his name was Randy Hoover. I could hit a grounder or fly ball and he could scoop it right up. When Randy would try to throw it back, it wouldn't go ten feet. I hit him a ground ball and he did a good job fielding it, when he took it out of the glove and started to throw it back, I yelled at him to hold it. Randy looked at me really funny. I told him to take the glove off his left hand and throw me the ball with his left hand. He threw it really well. I asked him why he was using that glove when he was a lefty. He said he didn't know he was left handed, and the glove belonged to his uncle. I told him to tell his mother to get him a glove that fit on his right hand. Randy turned out to be a good pitcher. Well, we worked out that summer two or three days a week. Some days we had five or six kids, some days we had as many as eight. When I say we, I mean me and two of the local dads who agreed to help me. (Bob Resler and Micky Johnson) It didn't take me very long to realize that they were two of the finest men I have ever known, and friends that I hold dear to me.

Grandpa's Stories

The Berryhill Warriors and me

Well, the spring of 1968 it was no longer just play. We were entered in the Westside League of Peewee C, 8 year olds. We had 14 boys, two coaches, and me the manager. Our name was the Berryhill Warriors. Our uniform was tennis shoes, blue jeans, numbered T-shirt and ball caps. Of our 14 Warriors, 5 or 6 could catch a ball, 4 or 5 could throw a ball, and about 7 of them could hit the ball.

We had a pretty good year, we won most of our games and lost a few. We wound up winning second place out of eight teams. The third game of the season, David White our center fielder was at bat. The pitcher walked him. Upon the umpire calling ball four, he told David to go to first base, that he had walked. David looked up at him and said, "No sir, our coach doesn't want us to walk, he wants us to hit the ball." In game four, Kelly Jones our right fielder was taking his turn at bat and the opposing pitcher threw him three perfect strikes. Kelly came back to the dugout mad as a hornet, looked up at me and says, "Coach, that umpire called me out and none of those balls were at my knees or shoulder. They were right here," and Kelly pointed to his belt buckle. Boy, we had some good times.

One game Kevin Mattison was playing right field and a fly ball was hit in his direction. I looked at Kevin to see if he had seen the ball hit to him. He was down on his knees looking at the ground. I yelled out his name and he looked up, located the ball, and made a beautiful catch, the ball was hit straight at him. His ball glove appeared to explode. Clover leaves flew everywhere. Midway through the season I told Dean Miller that I was going to move him to third base. Dean was a bright young boy who was our second best pitcher at that time. Dean had a gun for a right arm (that means he could really bring it, or throw the ball really hard if you're not hip to baseball lingo). Dean looked at me with a real serious look on his face and said, "Coach, where is third base?"

Year two, or Peewee "B" as we called it, was a great year for the Warriors. We won our league and the Tulsa City Play Offs. We were City Champions. We were a very fortunate team, like I said earlier. I had two great coaches. We had the boys hitting, throwing, and catching like professionals, well, almost that good. We had all of our boys return to play but one. Boyd Maxwell fell out of his attic and broke his arm. He came back to play a few years later. We had one kid who loved to play in the outfield but didn't like to take his turn at bat, Kenny LaBarge. In one game a long fly ball was hit to him, as he started back to catch it, five or six ball caps fell off his head. Yes, I said five or six. Kenny had to stop and gather them all up, re-stack, and put them back on before he proceeded to retrieve the ball. It would be needless to say that hit became a home run. Kenny had qualities that none of our other boys had. He was totally immune to poison ivy, so he became the best foul ball finder in the state. Kenny could also find snakes, baby rabbits, balls that had been lost for five or six years and old rusty pocket knives. Sometimes he would come back to the bench and unload before he had retrieved the foul ball.

Parents, we had the cream of the crop. Most of them were extremely good to help us keep our field mowed and in good condition, especially Sam Hester. Some were excellent side line coaches, sure to tell us where we were screwing up.

Harry Morton, Harry was David White's grandfather. David was the best center fielder in Tulsa for his age. Harry said he would buy the drinks (cold pop) when we won. Harry had half the money in Tulsa, he was on the Tulsa Metropolitan Planning Commission for many years, a retired vice-president of DX Refinery, Sun Oil as it is known today. He had a Tulsa City Park named after him at one time. One day I put David in to pitch a couple of innings. After the game Harry came over to me and said, "Oh Connie, I sure hope you aren't planning on making a pitcher out of David. When he gets in the Major Leagues it would break his heart to only get to play every four or five days." Perry Brown, now there was a good one. Perry was the grandfather of Sammy Hester, our left fielder, and sometimes third baseman. We were playing in the City Playoffs against Jerry Webber's team when the score keeper approached the umpire in charge and told him that we had an ineligible pitcher on the mound. This wasn't true of course, but the umpire notified me that he was forfeiting the game to Marshall, Jerry's team. I told him that someone was in error and it would be very easy to figure out how many innings anyone had pitched. He looked at our score book which was kept by Jean Chism, the wife of our pastor at that time. He agreed that our book was much more legible than the official score book. I asked him to call the manager of the team we had played the night before, and he agreed. While we were gone to phone him, a young red headed umpire came up to the bleachers and was mouthing off about our team. Perry Brown, who was eighty-six at the time, socked him and knocked him into the third row of the bleachers. Sam Hester, his son-in-law and a few more of my parents quickly broke it up before Perry could do any more damage. Upon our return to the field the umpire, after seeing what had happened, called the game a forfeit. We were leading five to one in the third inning. I had no choice but to protest the call. A special meeting was called by the Tulsa City Baseball Commission to hear the protest. The Commission agreed with me that the Official Score Keeper had made an error, and the game would be played from the point of the called forfeit. As for the fracas in the bleachers, me and all my coaches were barred from the remainder of the City Playoffs. A bunch of the mothers of our team wanted to coach the remainder of the playoffs but I found some of the fathers that I thought would be better qualified. We won that game and eliminated Marshall but lost the following game as my coaches and I watched from outside the park.

Most of the opposing team parents were super also. We made many lasting friendships along the way. In one game we were playing, an argument erupted over a call that the umpire had made. I was trying to explain exactly what the rule book said regarding the call when this dad from the opposing team stated, "I don't give a d____ what that book says, I've been to Busch Stadium in St. Louis three times to see the Cardinals play, I know what I am talking about." We also met other coaches that we invited over to our house for dinner.

Year three or Peewee "A" we had another good year. We were practicing one evening and I told Johnny Reed to get in the batter's box. I looked around for him and couldn't find him. "Has anyone seen Johnny Reed?" I said. One of the boys said that he's over there in the back of my station wagon. I looked over there and called to Johnny, "What are you doing over there?" Johnny said, "I'm looking for the batter's box!" We were invited to come over to McClure Park and play a practice game with another team in our age bracket. When we got there I thought the park looked a little small, I asked the other coach if they played the fence for a home run. He looked at me and laughed, "Sure it is a home run, but I've only seen one ball hit out of here by this age boy." I said, "Really, we have about five or six that can hit it out of here." He laughed again. We had five home runs that day by five different kids. We had the last laugh. In one game Kevin Mattison was coming up to bat, I called time out and told him to lay the ball down the third base line and run as hard as he could. Kevin was a really good bunter. He did exactly that, he laid down a perfect bunt, and ran as hard as he could down the third base line. That was an easy out for our competition.

While I was managing our team I was on the City of Tulsa Baseball Commission, and was over the Chandler Park League. There was a team in that league of sixteen year olds that had the son of Gene Shell, the University of Tulsa's baseball coach, playing for them. One evening Gene came over and sat down by me and we talked a little about baseball. He said, "You know C. R., I watched your team play in the City Playoffs and I haven't figured out yet how you won it. Your kids don't play very good defense." I said, "Well Gene, I thought our kids were playing pretty good, but when you average fourteen runs a game, you don't have to play really

Grandpa's Stories

good defense. Besides that, when our starting lineup is all in the game, we do all right." Gene said, "Well C. R., I have to give you that, you do have a bunch of hitters."

We were playing a game that year and I asked Van Hamby if he would like to catch for a couple of innings. He replied, "Yes, coach I would." I said, "Have you got a cup on?" Van replied, "Yes sir, Mr. Layton, I have to take care of the family jewels you know."

We won our league that year but got beat in the City Playoffs. The next year just before we were ready to start the season a friend called from another league and wanted to play us a practice game. Some of you have heard of this man, Don Chandler. He was the kicker for the Green Bay Packers Football Team during their heyday. Don sounded sad to me as he told me about his team. He said they never won a single game last year and thought if his kids could play on the same field as our Warriors it would help them a lot. Being real sympathetic, I benched our best five players, and didn't bring them in until the next to the last inning. It was too late, and we lost the game. Don told me that he really appreciated me letting his team win. Little did he know that was not my intention when we started the game. Don's team won their league that year and wound up winning the City Playoffs.

Those were some fun years and I wouldn't trade them for anything, but I wouldn't do it again for anything. All the boys have grown to manhood now. All of them finished High School, and some of them went on to play college baseball, one went on to play professional baseball. If anyone ever approaches you and asks if you will manage a Peewee Ball Team, run, no seriously those will be very special moments in life that you will never forget.

Grandpa's Stories

A VERY UNUSUAL GIFT

The year was 1980 and my son Tom was going to Bacone College on a baseball scholarship. It was the seventh of April and my 46th birthday. My daughter Melody Joy was home for the weekend from the University of Oklahoma. Bacone's baseball team was playing that Saturday at Northeastern A & M in Miami, Oklahoma. My son Tom was scheduled to pitch. Tom had been having a very good year; his statistics were exceptionally good and in his baseball coach's words, "The pro scouts were drooling over him."

Tommy after Pitching Birthday Shutout and No-Hitter

As we entered the baseball park at Miami, Tom spotted us and came over to greet us. He gave his sister Melody, whom he had not seen in several weeks, a big hug, told his mother and me hello, and told me Happy Birthday. Tom said, "Dad, I have been so busy that I haven't had a chance to go birthday shopping. How would you like to have a no-hitter in your honor as your present from me?" I said Tom, "That would be a very good gift, but don't you think that would be a very tall order to fill?" Pitching a no-hitter is no easy task to perform.

Well you've probably figured out by now what the "Very Unusual Gift" was. Tom did pitch a no-hitter for me that day, his third no-hitter of the season. I was really proud of my son, but I would have been proud of him if he had failed to do it as long as he had done the best he could. Shortly after Tom graduated from Bacone he was drafted and signed by the Cincinnati Reds.

Grandma's Stories

REMEMBERING MY EARLY YEARS OF THE LATE 1930s & 1940s

By the time I was born in 1937 most of my relatives had died, or died shortly after. I don't remember much about them. I am writing this story about a few relatives I do remember and the neighbors I remember who lived by me in the 500 block of S. 37th W. Ave.

My mother, dad, and I lived at 516 S. 39th W. Ave. We had a little three room, white, shotgun house and across the street from us lived my grandmother Susan Rogers, my mother's mother, my mother's sister Nancy Jane Rogers, who we called Aunt Jenny, and mother's brother John Walker Rogers, my uncle John. The three of them lived in a house just like ours. I remember my mother took care of all of us.

Grandma Susan Rogers, Mom, George and Clifford Rogers

The thing I remember most about my grandma was she made wonderful quilts out of old wool suits. Grandma would let me help her "tack" them with green yarn. The only other thing I remember about her was she would lay a fork in the corner of the living room when she thought "a flood was on the way." The fork did something to let her know when it was time to leave for higher ground. The fork deal has always been a real mystery to me.

Grandma's Stories

Aunt Jenny, Mom, Grandma Rogers, Martha Jo, Clifford, me, George

My Aunt Jenny was always sick. I think she had epilepsy. Back in those days people would say someone was having a "fit." Every afternoon Aunt Jenny would give me a dime to go get her a Pepsi. I would get her the Pepsi and bring her back a nickel. She thought I was bringing her more money than she gave me because the nickel was larger than the dime. For entertainment Aunt Jenny would play her old crank Victrola. The records she would play were 78 rpms by Bob Wills, Ted Weems, etc. I now have her prized possession.

Uncle John was quite a guy! He thought he was a real ladies' man and I guess he was. He had many lady friends and was married four times. Mother would wash and finger wave his hair when he was going out on the town. When he came home from a date Mother would sometimes have to get the gum off the seat of his pants with ice and elbow grease. In later years he calmed down and changed his life by going to church, and he loved to go to Sunday afternoon singing conventions. Instead of giving our children candy he would bring them sacks of apples because he said "all kids have too much candy." He was always going to plant them an apple tree, but he died too soon.

On the north end and across the street from us lived a very nice old lady we called Granny Baldwin. Granny had white hair and a glass eye. At night she took the eye out and in the morning she would put the eye back in. Mrs. Baldwin made great soup and banana bread. My mom and I would eat with her quite often, she loved for us to come. Mrs. Baldwin made quilts by sewing strips of material on 12x12 inch newspaper blocks. She would then sew the blocks together to make a quilt. I got the whole sum of 25 cents to tear off the newspaper for her.

Grandma's Stories

On the south end of the street about four houses from us lived Mr. and Mrs. Bob Peacock. Mr. Peacock was the neighborhood barber and had a barber shop next door to their home.

Next door to the barber shop was the grocery store owned by Mr. and Mrs. Joe Perryman. One day I ran off and went to the store for a jar of sour pickles and some sour kraut. When I got home with them, my mother was very upset with me for running off. I don't have any idea how I paid for them.

The Satterfields lived the first house north of us. Mr. and Mrs. Satterfield had a daughter named Claudia who we called 'little red' because she had the most beautiful red hair. The thing I remember the most about them was they had the nicest house on the block. Mrs. Satterfield had beautiful chenille bedspreads with elaborate flower designs on them.

Rupert Furr lived next door to the Peacocks. Rupert's wife was Babe Peacock Furr. Rupert had a Western Swing Band who practiced at their house. I would sit on their front porch and listen to them. In later years Rupert became a preacher and pastored several churches and used his music for Christ.

Jack and Leah Peacock lived next door south of us. Every once in a while they went somewhere to a farm. When they came home they always brought home some homemade butter. They always made me a great bread and butter sandwich.

After we moved to 418 S. 37th W. Ave. I would go back and play with my girlfriend Laverne Brown. The Brown family lived next door to where my grandmother's old house was on 39th. Paul and Ruth Brown were La Verne's parents. Ruth made the best brown beans and fried potatoes. Ruth told La Verne and I that to make good beans you have to stir them every time you pass them. Paul bought the first television in the block. On Saturday night Paul would put the TV on the front porch and the neighbors could bring over their chairs and watch TV. The other thing Paul did was make a big sled for all the kids in the neighborhood to ride on. I don't remember what he pulled the sled with as very few people had cars.

Grandma's Stories

When I was a little girl all our neighbors would visit and help each other. I lived on 39th W. Ave from the time I was 3 until I was 8 when we moved to 37th. I lived on 37th W. Ave. until I got married in 1957.
March 22, 2000

MOTHER WAS A LADY

Mother

There was a song written in 1895 by Edward B. Marks and Joseph W. Stern titled, "Mother was a Lady." The title of the song was the description of my mother. When I was a little girl Mother sang this song to me. My mother's name was Martha Lucinda Rogers Roberson. Mother was born August 12, 1903, in Stone County, Virginia. Mother married my father, Hollis Roberson, November 24, 1923, in Nocona (Montague County), Texas.

Mother was a little plump; she had beautiful long black hair that was down to her waist or more. Some of the ways she wore her hair were braided and wrapped around her head, in a bun on the back of her head, in a pompadour, or rolled up on a "rat." Mother had a big supply of black bobbie pins and large hair pins. Mother had a beautiful smile and clear black eyes.

My father died when I was eleven years old so my mother was everything to me. I was an only child, so it was just the two of us. Mother taught me about all the important things in life. I learned to love people, have compassion, be honest, and to always pay my bills. Most importantly, Mother taught me to love God and to live my life to the best of my ability.

When I was small, Mother would rock me and sing to me. We would rock and the rocking chair would move across the old wood floor. We would have to get up and move the rocker back to where we started from. I was too old and too big, but we both loved it. Mother would brush my long black hair which I also loved. When I was sick, Mother would cut an apple across the middle and scrape the apple out with a spoon. This made the apple almost like applesauce. It was wonderful.

Mother and me

Mother was extremely smart and could spell anything. Mother never really got to go to school as they had to work in the cotton fields and they moved a lot. I think she went through eighth grade, but she missed a lot during the year while working in the fields.

Before my dad died, Mother would turn the collars and cuffs of his white dress shirts when they were frayed. His shirts would look like new again. When my dad died, Mother went to work at The Hotel Tulsa laundry at 3rd and Cincinnati in downtown Tulsa.

When Mother got a vacation, she would teach the junior boys at Bible School. In my mind I can still see her walking down the road carrying her supplies to Home Gardens Assembly of God Church. At other times, she would go to youth camp and wash dishes.

Mother could make any day a party. On Valentine's Day we always had red jello made in the same bowl. It was a dark blue bowl that was white on the inside. (The bowl got broken by my son when he was young.) Sometimes we would really splurge and get one Pepsi, one small sack of Fritos, and one Baby Ruth candy bar that Mom would cut in small pieces. That was a real party. Sometimes for supper we would get a hunk of longhorn cheese. We would open the white butcher paper on the table which became our tablecloth. We would have cheese, crackers, and onion; what a feast! Our main treat was going "loopity loop" on the street car and getting a 5 cent ice cream cone before going home.

One Halloween Mother bought us a pressed paper jack-o-lantern which we would put in the front window. I still have the jack-o-lantern

Grandma's Stories

and my husband and I still put it in our window. For Christmas, we would walk to the Christmas tree lot and buy a small tree. We didn't have the money for a big tree or a car to carry it home in. Mother would carry the tree home and put it on a small table she had covered with a white sheet. By putting the tree on the table it made us a large tree or so we thought. Mother would put cotton around the bottom of the tree so we could have snow. We also put up a big paper bell in the middle of the living room hung on twisted red and green crepe paper.

When Mother was making biscuits or pie crust, she would get her big bowl of flour, make a hole in the middle of the flour, put the rest of her ingredients in the hole and mix in just enough flour with her hands. She would pinch off just enough for a biscuit or roll out the pie crust with her rolling pen my dad's father made her. I never remember the flour bowl being empty. She always had flour in the bowl and would cover it with a towel when she wasn't using it. Mother made the best and most beautiful cream pies. The real meringue would stand up about two inches tall on top of her pies. We had a large earthenware platter that Mother would beat the egg whites on. The egg whites were beaten with a fork. Mother would hold the platter almost upright, just about the time I thought they were going on the floor she would make a big sweep under them and keep beating them. When we had a pie supper at church, the old men would put their money together to buy the pie Mother had made for me to take. I hated it because I had to eat with them.

I can remember a time when Mother only had two dresses, one lavender and one pink. The dresses were just alike, open down the front with a collar, short sleeves and big white "pearl" buttons. Her dress was always fresh and clean. Mother and the other ladies in our neighborhood saved feed and flour sacks which they would trade with each other to have enough alike to make a dress. The pink and lavender dresses were not made of sacks.

When I was about twelve years old Mother had to have two operations. This was the only time I can remember Mother ever taking a nickel from anyone. It broke Mother's heart to do this, but she had no other choice. We had to take state aid for about eight weeks. When the case worker came to see if Mother was able to go back to work, Mother told her that the lady across the street gave her 50 cents for watching her little boy. You guessed it; they took the 50 cents out of her last check. It is hard to believe anyone would be that honest. It really made a big impression on me.

We lived by a lady who was always trying to kill herself. I don't know how Mother knew when she would do this, but Mother always made her fresh grape juice. When Mother took the juice to her, sure enough the lady would be sitting in front of her gas stove with the gas turned on. Mother always talked her out of it.

Mother loved her grandchildren, Melody and Tommy, more than anything. Melody loved it when Mother came to our house. They would sit on the floor and turn the toy box over and play. They would go over to Mark Twain School and play on the playground equipment, then they would take a walk through the underpass from the school under Charles Page Blvd. Once Mother even gave Melody a stick of butter to eat "because she loves it." When Tommy was born Mother was sick and couldn't pick him up. We would put Tommy on Mom's lap and she would play and talk to him.

The best memory I have of Mother is her walking through the house singing her favorite song, a hymn, For He is so Precious to Me. The chorus is as follows:
> For he is so precious to me
> For he is so precious to me
> Tis heaven below,
>   my redeemer to know,
> For he is so precious to me.

Mother with her Friend, Mr. Rose

Not one time did I ever hear Mother complain or say, "I wish things were different." By her life, she said it's not what you have, but how you live with what you have.

Grandma's Stories

I'm writing this story about a lady who was everything a lady should be. Mom was the greatest. I will always love her. I hope my children will think about me when I'm gone like I do her. I'm also writing this so our children and grandchildren can know about her. Mother was a lady in every respect. I never heard her say a bad word about anyone. She always had that big smile.

Mother died January 1, 1968, after being sick about seven years. She had a brain tumor and had two brain operations that left her paralyzed. Mother is buried at Woodlawn (really Woodland) Cemetery in Sand Springs, Oklahoma.

MY DAD

I'm writing a story about my dad who I didn't think I knew enough about to write. I woke up at 2.30 Wednesday morning remembering many things about him that I had forgotten.

Daddy and Mom

My dad's name was Hollis Roberson. He was a short, fair complexioned Irishman who had red hair. I remember him being as meek as a lamb, but I have been told that he was rough and tough and could make even a big man do what he thought was right.

Daddy was an impeccable dresser. I don't ever remember seeing him without a white dress shirt and tie. Daddy always wore a hat cocked over on one side of his head. I have a picture of my mom and dad in a row boat and even then he was dressed in a white shirt and hat.

My dad worked for the City of Tulsa, as a street sweeper in the 1940s. A street sweeper was a man who actually pushed a large broom to clean the streets of Tulsa. To get paid Daddy would have to go downtown to City Hall. I always went with him and he would ask Mother to "fix me up real pretty." Mother would get me all dressed up and off Daddy and I would go to catch the streetcar. I was my daddy's pride and joy and he always wanted to show me off.

My dad used Prince Albert tobacco to roll his own cigarettes, and he never put a cigarette out without lighting another one first. I thought it was great fun rolling the cigarettes for him. One time I found a tool called a brace and bit, and being the inquisitive little girl that I was I asked him what it was for. Instead of explaining what the tool was for, he showed me how to use it by drilling a hole in the kitchen door facing, then he let me do it, not just once but several times.

Me with Daddy

I only remember going with my daddy two places other than after his paycheck. One night he took me to the Brownie Father and Daughter Dinner at Mark Twain School. Mother fixed green beans for us to take in her Jewel Tea Casserole Bowl. I still have and use the bowl. The only other place I recall was Daddy taking my mother and I to an Ice Show at the Coliseum. A beautiful couple was skating to the music of Somewhere Over the Rainbow, and he told me that was his favorite song.

The biggest thing I remember was that my daddy ran a gambling hall in a hotel on Archer Street in downtown Tulsa. Mother and I both hated for him to do this, but it was like he was hooked and couldn't quit. A few times there would be a small article in the newspaper about Little Red and his gambling hall. I believe daddy probably bought the police off as he was not bothered very often, and he had his <u>business</u> several years. Daddy had a partner who we called Peg Leg George. I can recall one time I was told that Daddy caught a man cheating and pushed him down the stairs, breaking his arm. The man would not tell what had happened as he didn't want my daddy mad at him. Sometimes we had money and sometimes we didn't. If we had money Daddy would stand in the front door counting it. I have always been reluctant to talk about this part of my dad's life, but now I finally felt like I could write about it. Even though I hated for Daddy to do this I loved him and I know he loved me. He traded jewelry for gambling debts and one day he came home and gave me a lovely ruby ring. I might have seemed young for such a thing but my dad would have given his life for me. I wore the ring every day until I gave it to my daughter on her sixteenth birthday.

Daddy with Grandpa William Abner Roberson

Daddy died at St. Johns Hospital March 20, 1949 of congestive heart failure. I was only 11 years old at the time of his death. After my mom died I found two discharges for my dad. He was in the Army in World War I. I don't know if he got discharged and was called back, or if he volunteered to go back. I also received a letter from President Johnson saying he had been a hero, but all his war records were burnt so we have no reasons for his two discharges or his heroism.

Editor's Note: Since this writing, Grandpa Layton has established that Hollis Roberson was not an Irishman.

March 2003

UNCLE JOHN WALKER ROGERS

Uncle John was a different sort of fellow, but a real good man. Uncle John was born February 3, 1895 in Scott County, Virginia and died March 1, 1970 in Tulsa, Oklahoma. He was a Veteran of World War I. He made his living as a house painter and wallpaper hanger.

I remember when I was a little girl Uncle John moved back to Tulsa from Stockton, California. It was a great thrill getting to go down to the Union Depot and waiting for his train to come in. I believe he moved back to Tulsa to be nearer my mom after my dad died. He lived with us and helped us. I had no other uncles or aunts.

Grandma's Stories

Grandma with Cousins: Martha Jo, George, Eddie, Clifford, and me

Uncle John was a big handsome guy with black wavy hair. I never knew a man who had so many lady friends and I know he was married at least three times. His first wife Dora was John Edward's (Eddie) mother, Marie was Martha Jo's mother, and his third wife was Ethel and they had no children. Martha Jo was named after my mother. I remember Ethel, the lady he married last, because of her beautiful red hair.

Uncle John with Marie and Martha Jo

I remember when he would go courtin' Mom would finger wave his hair. In his later years he used the black Grecian formula on his hair. One night when he came home he had sat down on chewing gum and of course it had stuck to his pants. He wanted Mother to get it off which she did by freezing it with ice and pulling it off.

Uncle John liked to go dancing and he liked to shoot pool. He had his own pool cue and he always took it with him. In his later years, he went to church a lot and he loved good Gospel music.

When I was a young girl my biggest frustration with him was when he hid my radio. I could not think of what I could have done to make him so mad at me. I would call Mother at work and tell on him. Mother would say, "Tell him I want to talk to him." She would tell him in no uncertain terms to give me my radio that the house was ours and he didn't tell me what to do or bother my stuff.

After I got married, Uncle John continued to live with Mother. Then Mother had a brain tumor and was never the same again. We brought her to our house. While she was at home and sick Uncle John took great care of her along with the neighbor ladies. After her death we continued to let him live in her house for several years until he brought in bee hives

Grandma's Stories

and the neighbors complained. He wouldn't get rid of the bees so we had to tell him to move.

After having a minor car wreck Uncle John's mind really changed and he thought someone was after him all the time. He was living in a small apartment and sometimes he would call and tell us someone was spying on him and could he come over to our house and stay a few days because he thought for sure our house was the only place he was really safe.

Uncle John loved our children and would bring them a big sack of apples. He would always say that when the children were bigger he was going to plant them an apple tree. There was not to be any candy for them as candy was not good for them.

Uncle John with his Son, Eddie and Mary Martha, Eddie's Daughter

There came a time when he wanted to give me all his money for "safekeeping" but I wouldn't take it as I was afraid he would accuse me of taking it. His mind wasn't the best at that time. This money was to be used for his funeral expenses. Unknown to me he gave it to a man in Muskogee at the VA Hospital. After he died we began to look for his money and found the name of the man he had given it to. It was in his "safe" (his cigar box). I called the gentleman at the hospital and he said he would give me the money except for the amount of the taxes he would owe on it. There was barely enough money to bury him, even though we gave him the lot where he is buried. He died at the VA hospital and we would go visit him often and he would want Connie to rub his legs as it would relax him. We buried him beside my mom and dad at Woodlawn (really Woodland) Cemetery in Sand Springs, OK. We always decorate his grave every Memorial Day along with the others.

Uncle John was much more than an Uncle to me even though he was ornery. I loved him very much.

Grandma's Stories

REMEMBERING THE GOOD OLD DAYS

This story is about how life was when I was a little girl, in the late 1930s, and the early 1940s, and about the people and the things they did to make life better.

No one I knew had a car and so a lot of services were provided by a person coming to your home, such as the ice man, and milk man, etc. I remember my mom had a wooden icebox which had three doors. One side had one big compartment with shelves. The other side had two compartments. The top compartment was for the ice, and the compartment under the ice also had shelves. Mother had an ice card that was divided into quarters. Each quarter on the card was a different color with different amounts ranging from twenty-five pounds to one hundred pounds printed on the different colors. Mother would put the card in the front screen door with the amount of ice she wanted sticking up. The ice man would drive up, look at the card, pick up his metal tongs and get the block of ice. The ice would be brought in through the back door and put in the ice box. We had an ice pick which we would use to chip ice to put in a glass if we wanted ice water, tea, or a Pepsi.

I remember the milk man would bring milk to a lot of our neighbors. I don't remember Mom buying milk from him, but we only lived four doors from the neighborhood grocery store. I do remember the milk man coming to our home after I got married and had children. Mr. Satterfield, worked for Meadow Gold Milk Co., was our milk man. We always bought two, two and one half gallon cartons with the built in spout. Our son went through milk in a hurry.

The man I remember most was the farmer with the horse drawn wagon. The horse was old, slow, and had a swayed back, but it pulled the wagon faithfully every summer. The old horse would pull the farmer and his wagon down each street with their bell ringing to let the people know they were coming. The people who wanted to buy vegetables would go out to the wagon and buy whatever the farmer had grown that was in season.

Grandma's Stories

Mom would buy green beans which she canned, corn and tomatoes, etc. Everything he sold was so good and fresh. Best of all were his watermelons. I remember he would always ask us if we wanted him to "plug" it. He would get his long knife and cut out a triangle in the middle. The farmer would always give me the plug to taste. The watermelons were always good, but they were much better after Mother put them in the icebox to let them get "real cold," as my mom would say. I believe Mom paid twenty-five cents for them.

I also remember the products Mother bought at the grocery store that had the "free gift" inside the box. Oatmeal had dishes which some are worth a lot of money today. There were towels in boxes of soap. At first the company put solid colored towels in the boxes, but soon started giving striped and flowered towels. In the 1960s and 1970s Bonus put towels in soap. Bonus soap was not the soap Mom got towels in. Duz put glasses and dishes in soap from 1929-1978 but I don't remember this.

The ladies thought you had to have Mrs. Stewarts bluing to put in the second tub of rinse water after washing the white cloths to make them <u>really</u> white. I believe there was a quiet competition among the ladies as to who had the whitest cloths on their clothes lines. Some of the ladies who had white hair rinsed it in the bluing, often their hair would be a little too blue. I had a grade school music teacher, Mrs. Cunningham, whose hair was always blue. My mom and I made a Magic Salt Crystal Garden out of bluing, coal, water, mercurochrome, ink, and salt.

I remember the white margarine with a button of red food coloring on top. When the coloring was mixed in the margarine it gave it a yellow butter color. I believe some people were afraid of the red food coloring so the margarine company would put it there if you wanted to use it. I always wanted the job of mixing it.

The Jewel Tea Co. salesman came around and the ladies could get dishes for trading with them. I don't remember how that was done, but I have some of Mother's dishes.

Flour and chicken feed came in print sacks which the ladies would trade with each other in order to have enough alike to make a "feed sack dress." Some products came in white sacks which made wonderful tea towels, which some ladies embroidered. Mom embroidered a "set" of towels with each towel having a different design and a different day of the week on them.

At one time all sheet and pillow cases were white and to make the pillow cases pretty the ladies would iron on a transfer pattern and then embroider them. Some of the ladies would make lace by crocheting or tatting to put on the bottom of the pillowcases. My mother made the most beautiful tatting lace which she put on all kinds of linens.

One of the most fun things I ever did was make "roll your own" cigarettes for my daddy. I used white tobacco paper that came in an orange package, and Prince Albert tobacco. The cigarettes were rolled on a red, steel cigarette roller, and then the ends were trimmed.

The last thing I'm writing about was the old push lawnmower. There was no such thing as a gas or electric mower. The good thing about mowing was that most yards where I lived were small.

I'm not really sure those were the good old days, but as I look back I don't remember ever hearing my mom complain about their life. Maybe the reason they didn't complain was because the ladies before them had it a lot harder than they did. I'm actually glad to have a "ice box" that makes ice, automatic washer and dryer, dishwasher, and a garage door opener. I'm really thankful for a gas riding lawn mower with a great guy to ride it for me.

June 2001

GRANNY BALDWIN

When I was a little girl my mother and I lived at 516 S. 39th W. Ave. We lived by a widow lady whose name was Baldwin. Granny, as we called

Grandma's Stories

her, was a sweet, stout lady with white hair. I was always intrigued by Granny as she had a glass "eye" which she would take out at night and put in a box.

I loved to rock in Granny's old cane back rocking chairs, and look at her wonderful photo albums. Mrs. Baldwin supplemented her income by selling quilts she made from cotton material, men's ties, or men's wool suits. I can remember the quilts called strip quilts which were strips of material she would sew on 12 by 12 inch square blocks of newspaper. The squares were then sewn together to make a quilt. I was paid a quarter to pull the newspaper off the quilt.

Mrs. Baldwin loved for my mother and I to come to her house for dinner, which was always homemade soup, apple salad, and pumpkin bread. When the front door was opened we were always greeted by the wonderful smell of the pumpkin bread baking, but what I really liked was the apple salad. I had never had apple salad like she made, and I don't know anyone but me who makes it now.

The first Thanksgiving after my husband and I were married I made Granny's apple salad and took it to my mother-in-law's for dinner. It was a big hit. After 46 years of marriage I still make it for Thanksgiving and Christmas. When we go to a dinner where everyone brings a dish I am often asked to "bring the wonderful apple salad you make." I don't know why I don't make it more often as it is so easy and good. The apple salad is a little tart, but that is what makes it so good.

Following below is Granny Baldwin's Apple Salad Recipe.

To make the salad I use Delicious Apples which I cut into small size bites, and for each apple I use I make the following dressing:

1 well beaten egg
4 tablespoons sugar
4 tablespoons vinegar

In a small sauce pan mix together the above and cook slowly, stirring often so the egg doesn't lump. When the dressing is done it should be like a thin pudding.

Pour the dressing over the chopped apples, and add some chopped pecans. (The pecans are optional.)

January 2003

MY VERSION OF *THE VIEW FROM THE FOLDING CHAIRS*

At our last reading get together at the Parks' house, Beth loaned me her book *The View from The Folding Chair*. I don't remember sitting in a folding chair very often but I may have in Sunday School. The story is so much like I remember my childhood that I decided to write my own memories of my childhood using this book as a guide. The book has several memories that I relate to, but, not necessarily in the order as I remember mine.

Hard Times: Mom had just taken a hot apple pie out of the oven when a hobo or bum as they were sometimes called came to our front door very hungry. Mom told him to sit down on our front porch and she would get him something. I can almost see Mom carrying a big piece of the hot apple pie in one hand and a large, cold glass of milk in her other.

Coupons: We had to have coupons or stamps for almost everything we bought. Two things I remember well were meat and lady's hose. Mom kept the Chote children, but their mother never gave my mom any stamps although Mother fixed their meals. One night Mom cooked a small amount of meat and put a small portion on each plate, and I do mean small. Toney, the youngest girl reached over to Mom's plate and took Mom's meat. Mother never said a word and didn't even act like she saw her. The other thing I remember most was the ladies who mended hose at Kress. It was extremely hard for ladies to buy nylons.

Service Men: In our front window Mom had a memorial flag which had a picture of her nephew John Edward Rogers who we called Eddie. The

Grandma's Stories

picture was of him in his navy uniform, with the words U.S. Navy printed above the picture. Another cousin of mine was George Rogers who was a prisoner of war in Korea for thirty-one months.

Sadie: In the book, a white enamel commode with a white lid was called Sadie. We didn't have a name for ours, but we had one. We also had a path out back to an outhouse with a Sears catalog. I remember at Halloween the neighborhood boys would sometimes turn it over.

Washing Machines: We had a wringer machine with two rinse tubs. After running the clothes through the wringer they were hung out on the clothesline with wooden clothespins to dry. When the clothes were dry they were brought in to either fold or sprinkle for ironing the next day.

Tinfoil: We saved tinfoil for the war effort and turned it in at school. I can almost feel my fingers pulling the foil off a piece of gum wrapper.

Christmas Trees and Presents: Each year Mom and I walked to the Christmas tree lot and bought a small tree, and Mom would carry it home. The tree was lovingly placed on a small table and we covered the base of the tree with a white sheet. The sheet became our snow. Mom would lay the lights on the floor and plug them in to make sure all the bulbs worked before putting them on the tree. Mom's main thing were the icicles. The icicles had to be put on one at a time and hung very straight. After Christmas we took the icicles off very carefully so we could save them for next year. We hung twisted red and green crepe paper from corner to corner of the living room with a big red paper bell hanging in the middle. We didn't have hardly any presents, but we had a lot of love and happiness.

Bread and Butter Sandwich: In the book it talks about putting sugar on their sandwich. I never put sugar on mine, but I ate a lot of bread and butter sandwiches. My next door neighbors were the Jack Peacock family. The Peacock's would go to a farm where some of their family lived and when they came returned home they always brought fresh churned butter with them. They always invited me over for a sandwich.

Grandma's Stories

The author of this book speaks of riding a train, but I got to ride a streetcar, in fact, everywhere I went. I loved them.

School: Mark Twain elementary, which is located between 41st and 42nd streets, on Charles Page Boulevard. Some school events were parties, programs, and on May Day we wound the May Pole which was great fun. I remember getting the weekly readers which I loved. The main thing I remember was our fifth grade teacher Mrs. Nesbitt who would always ask how many of us went to Sunday School. Those who did would raise their hands and she would count and write the number on the black board.

Deaths: The book talks about being a child and the ordeal of dealing with death. My dad died when I was barely eleven years.

Graduation: When we graduated from Central High School all the girls had beautiful white dresses which we wore under our graduation gowns. At the ceremony there was the prayer, the long boring speeches, and passing out of our diplomas which took forever as over seven hundred graduated.

Victory Garden: Mr. Giles, the principle of Mark Twain, gave anyone who wanted to have a garden a small section of the schoolyard for a garden. Several families took advantage of this opportunity. This food could either be eaten or canned. Mom canned some things, but they had to be placed in the jars just so. Each jar was to be admired.

Phones: We had an old black phone that sat on a table but we had a four party line. Sometimes it was hard to get to use your phone. If you had an important call to make the person talking would let you use the line if you were lucky.

Stilts and Rubber Guns: My girlfriend Deanna Hall and I were about the only girls on our street so we played with the boys. My cousin Clifford Rogers made Deanna and I rubber guns so we could play with the boys. Those rubber bands could really sting when they hit you.

Movies: Saturday afternoons we went to either the Star or the Harmony theater in Sand Springs where we saw a news reel, a cartoon, and coming attractions, before the main film. We watched a serial, which was a

Grandma's Stories

continued adventure story. The serial always ended where you would want to come back the next week to see what happens next.

Practice Air Raids: We would have to stay in the house and close our curtains tight so the light would not show out. I don't remember what the signal for doing this was but I know there was a certain signal. I remember when we were at school and the siren went off we got under our desk, folded our hands above our heads for protection. In a conversation with my friend Jean Marie Rogers she told me that her dad Buss Wooldridge was an Air Raid Warden for the Civil Defense. His job was to go out looking for "bombs" which were paper triangles dropped from a plane. People in Mr. Wooldridge's area would bring the bombs to him to be turned in with the location they were found. We believe the signal for the Air Raid drill was given from the oil refinery.

Seasons: Spring, gardening; Summer, Bible School Camp; Fall, school started; Winter, ice skating on the pond by Roosevelt Jr. High.

Parades: We went to a lot of parades downtown, usually Christmas, Rooster Day, Veteran's Day, etc. My husband and I were talking about parades and we could remember that anyone who wanted to could join in at the end could do so by walking or riding horseback. By having the horses at the end, bands and other paraders didn't have to walk through horse droppings.

Something we remembered that was not in the book was the saving of string. Before meat was prepackaged it was wrapped in white butcher's paper and tied with string. The string was saved and rolled into a ball and used at a later date for anything that needed to be tied.

January 2004

Grandma's Stories

THE OLD HOUSE I GREW UP IN

When I was a little girl I lived in a "shotgun house" with my mother Martha Rogers Roberson and my daddy Hollis Roberson. Just across the street was another house exactly like ours. Grandma Susan Alexander Rogers, Aunt Jenny, and my Uncle John lived in it. For those who don't know what a shotgun house is, it's three rooms from front to back. According to Connie, it was called that because you could open the doors and shoot a shotgun thru the front door and the bullet would go out the back door without hitting anything in the house. The purpose was to allow air to flow through. Mother took care of us in both houses. It wasn't long before Grandma and Aunt Jenny died and I think Uncle John moved to California.

Mom with Grandma Rogers in front of Shotgun House

After a while Mother and Daddy bought a big four room house two blocks away which needed a lot of work. They were going to do the work themselves, but as fate would have it Daddy died leaving just Mother and me. Back then insurance was unheard of.

Mother went to work at the Hotel Tulsa doing its laundry. It was a hard hot job but we had to eat. She made the whole sum of .25 cents an hour and I think we got the sum of $54 a month from the Government because my dad was a Veteran of WWI.

The house Mom and Dad bought was at 418 South 37th West Avenue. The house had no water inside but we had a faucet out in the front yard. All the water we used came from that faucet. The family across the street got all of their water from our faucet for everything including the baths for seven kids.

Grandma's Stories

We had a gas kitchen stove in the kitchen and one small gas radiant stove in the living room. At night Mother would put a brick in the front of the living room stove, let it get hot and wrap it in a towel, and put it in the bed to warm the bed.

For electricity we had a light bulb hanging from a wire in the center of each room. It had a switch on the bulb holder where you turned it off and on. We had a hole between the kitchen and back porch which Mom would throw something over and we would just step over it.

For a bathroom we had a potty, or chamber pot, which was also called the "slop jar." Mom would empty it every morning in the outhouse. (Now they are called PortaJohns.)

In the kitchen, we had no cabinets, just a faucet hanging on the wall., only cold water. We would fill a pan with water and put it on the stove to heat it to wash the dishes and anything else we needed to clean. After I met Connie and he saw our plight, he got his stepdad and they came and fixed it all. They fixed the hole, built cabinets, and put a sink in the cabinet top. And never charged us a penny. What two great men!

At some point the City made everyone hook onto the sewer, so we got an indoor bathroom and put it in the back bedroom. Before we got the indoor bathroom we would take turns taking our Saturday night baths in a number two wash tub. Me first and then Mom. We would bring in a bucket of water and put it on the stove to get it warm and then pour it in the tub.

Connie won a used television at work on a raffle and gave it to Mother. We didn't have air conditioning, we just opened the window and had a big black Emerson fan.

After we were married Connie completely rewired the house. He took out the old knob and tube wiring and ran new Romex wiring to each room adding wall receptacles to every wall and a wall switch for the overhead light fixtures.

Now we have all the comforts we could want. I guess we really don't want for anything. At one time my oldest grandson said all this house really needs is a big screen TV which we now have.

CLANG, CLANG, CLANG WENT THE TROLLEY

When I was a little girl, we rode the trolley, or as we called it, the street car. The street car was the most popular means of transportation for the people living on the Sand Springs line, which is now along Charles Page Boulevard. Most people did not own a car.

Mr. Charles Page started the street cars so more companies would come to Sand Springs and so the people could get to work. The street cars were also a means to help finance his orphanage and his widow's colony: I was told the street cars started May 10, 1911, but as this was before my time I don't know if that is correct. I remember the street cars being red with black numbers on them. The cars had advertising just above the windows; there were signs saying "Coloreds use rear."

There was one track beginning at Archer and Greenwood in Tulsa, running west to Sand Springs where it made a loop down Main Street to Broadway, on by the lake where it then paralleled itself along Charles Page Blvd. to just east of Newblock Park where the two tracks became one track again. Sometimes we would have to wait for a street car coming on the single track to get by so the street car we were on could continue.

From downtown Tulsa going west the streetcar went west on Archer St., curved around about Lawton St. where it went under the 3rd Street Viaduct. The street car would then follow the river going by Newblock Park, and at 33rd West Avenue where 3rd Street curved, it crossed over to the north side of 3rd Street and went on in to Sand Springs.

The stops where I got on going west were Parkview, Home Gardens, Vern, Glen, Medio, Lawnwood, Bruner, the Stockyards, Lake and the Sand Springs Greenhouse. The street car went on west to Main Street in Sand

Grandma's Stories

Springs where it circled north. The street car would stop at 2nd and Main Street before turning back east on Broadway. The waiting room was at McKinley and Broadway, where the street cars would stop before heading back to Tulsa. The next stop would be at the lake where, at one time, there was an amusement park with rides and animals. The lake was a wonderful place for swimming, baptizings, etc. This is where I was baptized as a child.

Going east, from where I got on at Parkview, were Hale, Joe, Newblock, Frisco, 3d Street, and on into Tulsa, going east on Archer to the end of the line at Greenwood Street, the street car would stop along the line on Archer at the downtown streets which were Denver, Cheyenne, Boulder, Main, Boston, and Cincinnati, then on to Greenwood Street.

Most stops had a three-sided waiting area with a wooden bench to sit on while waiting. The conductors had a schedule to keep and did so most of the time. The streetcar ran every twenty minutes and every ten minutes during busier times.

All throughout the night, it ran every hour. In Sand Springs, at Broadway and McKinley, and in Tulsa, at Archer and Boston, there were nice big waiting rooms where magazines, papers, candy, pop, and other things were sold. We never had the money to buy anything so we would pick out a comic book, set down on the floor by the comic book section, and read. No one ever got onto us for doing this. I imagine most comic books that were sold were a little bit used.

Just before the street car curved onto Main Street in Sand Springs was the Sand Springs Power and Water Co. Behind the plant, there was always a mist coming from the plant. We would always open the window and stick our arms out to get wet as we thought that was great fun. In the summer, it would cool us off as there was no air conditioning. I think as many adults as children did this.

If you wanted to get off at one of the stops, you would pull the cord running along the side of the street car above your head. There was a bell above the conductor's head that he would ring to let you know the street car was approaching.

Grandma's Stories

As a rule, most of the conductors were very friendly and they knew most of the riders by name. My favorite conductor was Mr. Stevens. My husband's favorite was Mr. Goff who is still living. The conductors wore black suits, white shirts, black bow ties, and black flat-top hats with a bill. On the front of the hat was a badge with the conductor's number on it. They wore a silver change holder on a black belt. They always looked so neat.

At the front of the car was a box on a stand that we dropped our nickel in. If we didn't have a nickel the conductor would give us change. When we went to school, we could buy a ticket that was less expensive. Newspapers were put on the street cars and the conductor would throw them off at some of the waiting areas so the paper boys could get the papers for delivery to their customers.

The seats had a back that would change depending on which direction the street car was going, so the passengers could face forward at all times. If you wanted to sit with your friends, you could have one seat forward and one seat backward, so you could face each other. Sometimes the cars were so full you had to stand up. The conductors would let people on as long as there was standing room.

The electric lines that powered the electric motors on the street car ran about ten feet above the street cars between Sand Springs and Tulsa with a long rod-type connector, called a trolley, from the car to the electric lines on both ends. When the conductor got to Greenwood, he would either reach out the front window or get off and change the trolley so the street car could go the other direction. Sometimes when the conductor would stop the street car, some kid would pull the connector down just to get the conductor's goat. I think maybe my husband did this a time or two. Another thing the boys would do was lay a penny on the track, so the street car would flatten it, and even lay caps from their cap gun so they would go bang, bang, bang.

I only remember one street car wreck and I was on it. It happened just west of Newblock Park where the Smith Sand trucks crossed the tracks. No one was killed, with only a few riders being hurt. I was probably hurt more

Grandma's Stories

than anyone else, but I didn't let anyone know because I didn't want to go to the hospital. At a later date, two men came to our house and gave Mom twenty-five dollars to get her to sign a release. They told her to get me some new shoes as all girls liked new shoes.

There was a regular rider who would sit on the bench at the front of the street car. The rider was Billy Bruner and everyone knew him. Billy was a big Indian who wore a big hat with a huge feather. Billy almost always had had too much to drink. I was afraid of him. My husband told me that Billy always gave money to children. I guess I never got that close to him.

For something to do, my mother and I would catch the street car and ride to Sand Springs. We would get off at 2nd and Main Street, go in the Glencliff dairy and get both of us a 5-cent ice cream cone. We would then get back on the next street car and ride all the way to Greenwood, stay on the car and ride back to Parkview where we would get off and walk home. We called that going "Loopity Loop." We would ride the whole distance, both have an ice cream cone all for a total of 30 cents.

The street cars meant everything to its riders as they were a lot of people's only means of transportation. We could walk to the street cars and then when we got off we could walk to where we were going. On Saturday afternoons the street car would take us to the Star Theatre in Sand Springs for the weekly serial. We could hardly wait for the next Saturday to see what happened next. On Sundays the street cars would take their riders to church. During the week, we rode the street car to Archer and Guthrie where we would get off and walk to Roosevelt Jr. High School. When we finally got old enough for high school, we rode the street car to Archer and Cincinnati where we would get off and walk to Central High School. If it was really cold we would get off at Boston, walk up to the railroad depot where we would walk through to Cincinnati to get warm and then on to Central High.

The street car was a great place of socializing. A lot of plans were made as to what we planned to do or where we could go or just to be with our friends. If someone was real ambitious some last minute homework could be done. The street car was my mother's means to get to work at the Hotel Tulsa laundry. Would you believe that you could even get a weather forecast on the street car? Of course, all you had to do was watch the National Bank of Tulsa building tower for the changing lights. If the light was green, we would expect fair weather. If it was red, we could expect to have bad weather. The street car was great for a lot of things.

When we heard they were taking the street cars out of service we were very sad. It was like losing an old friend. When the street cars were replaced by buses it was never the same. The street cars stopped running in 1955.

This story was written as I remember it about one of my favorite memories of my childhood and teenage years.

August 1998

MY DAYS AT MARK TWAIN ELEMENTRY SCHOOL

I went to Mark Twain Elementary School from the mid-40s to the early 50s, 1st through 6th grade. It is located between Forty-first and Forty-third W. Ave. and Charles Page Blvd. (which was called The Sand Springs Line) and Fifth St. We usually had about 20 kids in each class from kindergarten through the sixth grade. I have several friends from those school days that went on to Roosevelt Junior High, and Central High that I see at the Penny Park Reunion which is held each year on the first Saturday after Labor Day. It's nice to see them again.

Some of the teachers as I remember were Mrs. Nesbitt, Cutting, Sanders, Harris and of course the Principal Mr. Giles. Mrs. Harris was the science teacher who would slap the back of your hand with a wooden ruler for talking, etc. I don't remember much about Mrs. Sanders, but she was my fourth grade teacher. My favorite teacher was Mrs. Nesbitt who taught fifth grade. Every Monday morning Mrs. Nesbitt would ask how many children went to Sunday school and she would write the number on the

Grandma's Stories

blackboard. Our music teacher was Mrs. Cutting (AKA Mrs. Blue Head) because she put laundry bluing on her hair. I really liked her because I was into music big time and I played the piano. I remember Mrs. Cutting would make each child sing a few notes and she would decide if you were a bluebird or blackbird. If Mrs. Cutting thought you could sing, she called you a bluebird. If she didn't think you could sing, she called you a blackbird. I was always a bluebird, but it bothered me because my best friend was a blackbird and I felt sorry for her. I liked our gym teacher Miss Richey who was very tall and thin. My mother told me that Miss Richey said I always had the cleanest and whitest underwear she ever saw. At that time, we wore dresses and sat on the gym floor so sometimes our underwear would show. The last teacher I remember was Mrs. Hays, our librarian, who my mother almost got fired. One day Mrs. Hays left the room and I got up to sharpen my pencil. As I was walking to the sharpener I started to pass a boy who reached out and wrapped his legs around my legs and wouldn't let me go. Just about the time I drew back my fist to belt him in the mouth Mrs. Hays walked in and caught me. Instead of her getting on to him she spanked me! Mr. O. J. Giles was a great Principal who everyone loved. Each morning Mr. Giles stood on the front porch and greeted the children as they came in. At noon any second grader could go to Mr. Giles office and he would help them with their multiplication tables. When you learned them he gave you a $1.00 bill and wrote his name on it, I still have mine.

Grandma's Stories

The north part of the school ground was used for Victory Gardens. Anyone in the neighborhood who wanted to plant a garden could contact Mr. Giles who would assign you a plot of ground. Mom and I had a small garden, which supplied us with good, fresh vegetables.

We practiced for air raid drills by getting under our wooden desk and folding our hands on top of our heads. When the bells rang a certain way we knew it was for a fire or a fire drill. We would line up on the sides of the halls and go outside and stand with all our classmates and teacher.

Once a week we could buy victory stamps for war bonds, which were pasted in a booklet. When the booklet was full we turned them in for a War Bond. The kids were young but we were doing our part for the war effort.

Every week the people from the Tulsa Council of Churches would come to school and get the kids who wanted to go to Bible School. The old Home Gardens Assembly of God church building (the brown rock church located at the corner of Fifth Street and Forty-third Street) was where the Bible School was held. Nearly all the kids would go and I loved it.

Some of the kids were chosen to be safety patrols and our job was to "help" the little kids get across the street safely. We thought we were really big and important when we were given the white safety patrol belt with the "silver" badge on our shoulder. We got to ride a bus and go to Philbrook Art Center at the end of the school year for doing such a good job. We were given a small bottle of orange juice just before getting on the bus to go home.

We had several programs, plays, etc. Any of the kids who wanted to could participate in them, which was great fun. The highlight of the sixth

Grandma's Stories

grade graduation to me was the winding of the Maypole. I can still see the pole with all the light colored net hanging down from the top of the pole just waiting to be wound. The netting was pretty colors of white, pink, green, lavender, blue and yellow. With the music playing we went around and around weaving in and out, until the pole was covered with the net.

This story was written after I was given an invitation from Elizabeth Cochran, the Kindergarten teacher at the <u>new</u> Mark Twain School. I will be going for a tour of the new building and to visit her class. I am looking forward to this visit very much.

October 2004

THE PIANO

Several years ago, there was a young girl named Beverly who had long black hair and who was about eight years old. Beverly wanted more than anything to have a piano. That young girl was me. I was an only child and lived in a small, white house with my mother and daddy. The house we lived in was in Tulsa, Oklahoma on the Sand Springs line. I was the apple of my mother and daddy's eye, but they did not have the money for a piano or any other extras.

Playing on my Wedding Day

One day when I came home from school there was <u>MY</u> piano. Mother had found a piano that she could pay for a little at a time, and had someone deliver it for her. The piano was very old, very big, very black, and completely out of tune. Most people would have thought it was awful. To me the piano was not very big, very old, or very black. It was beautiful. I wouldn't have loved it more if it had been a new Steinway. My piano was the most important treasure I had.

Grandma's Stories

I would play the piano from early morning until time to go to school. After school, I played until bedtime. Our little living room became a concert hall or so I thought.

When I was a young teenager, about thirteen, I got a new Lester Betsy Ross spinet, but it wasn't nearly as big a thrill as my first piano. I still enjoy the piano and believe everyone should have something in their life like I loved my piano.

CHRISTMAS MEMORIES

C.R with Mom's Tree

Every year my mother and I would walk to the Christmas tree lot that was located on the south side of Charles Page Boulevard at the 3700 block. My mother and I would pick out a small tree that Mom could carry home as we didn't have a car to bring it home in, or the money to buy a large tree. We would put the tree on a small table covered with a white sheet and pretend that we had a tall tree on a snow covered mountain. We would decorate the tree with a string of lights and icicles. The bulbs were shaped like a Santa, house, snowman, or other Christmas object. The lights burned out many years ago, but I still have three of the old bulbs we still hang on our tree as decorations. My mother thought icicles had to be hung one at a time and straight down. I remember twisting red and green crepe paper together and hanging it from one corner of our living room to the other. We would then hang our red paper bell from the center of the crepe paper.

I still believed in Santa until I was about eight years old which is when I found a red wagon hidden behind our couch in the living room. I pretended not to see it, and never said a word. When Christmas morning rolled around I knew where it came from.

Grandma's Stories

I don't remember much about Christmas during my teen years. The first Christmas after I met my husband he gave me a beautiful black music jewelry box which I still have and use.

The first Christmas after we were married our beautiful daughter Melody Joy was born. Melody was the best Christmas present ever. We were supposed to go to my husband's parents' home for Christmas dinner. My husband's sister Jeri and her children were going be there along with my mother and Uncle John. I was supposed to make my famous chocolate mayonnaise cake, but I decided to have our daughter instead. My mother-in-law never let me forget her not getting the cake.

Manger Scene 60 Years Later

That same Christmas I wanted a nativity to put under our tree, but we didn't have the money to buy one. My husband who always wanted to please me went to Kress and bought a set of Christmas figures consisting of Mary, Joseph, and Jesus. The manger was made out of an orange crate that he talked the fruit stand owner out of. I still have my nativity which is put under our tree each year. When our son Tommy was old enough he wanted to put the nativity under the tree, and did so until he had his own home to decorate. Each year when we get our decorations down my husband will say, "I will buy you any nativity you want, that one can't last much longer." No new nativity for me, this one is special and among my most treasured possessions. Our tree would not be complete without it.

One Christmas morning when Tommy was about eight years old I woke up to a strange sound. I woke my husband and ask him what was that noise was I hearing. He said it sounded like an electric train to him. We peeked into the den and sure enough there sat Tommy playing with his train. We never said a word to him and went back to bed as if nothing happened.

When we got up the next morning there was the train all boxed up wrapped just the way it was when we put it under the tree. We never mentioned we knew he had already been playing with it until he was much older. Now about every Christmas we tease him about it.

Our "Decors"

One year just after we had finished putting out Christmas decorations in place our oldest grandson Thomas who was three years old came into our home and said, "Grandma, you have your 'decors' out." I think he meant decorations, but now we still put our "decors" out.

One year we went to Melody and Mike's for Christmas. All of Mike's family were there along with our family which made 26 people. We had a lovely dinner in their library. Melody had rented tables and covered them with bright red tablecloths which hung to the floor. The room was beautiful and the food delicious. Our granddaughter Maeve, and grandson Thomas, along with Mike's niece Erin served the meat. Each child had a platter of either ham, turkey, or roast. The children went around to each table serving the guest. I thought Melody was extremely brave to do this, but the children served each guest like a pro.

Some of our favorite things my husband and enjoy doing at Christmas are decorating out home inside and out. Most of our decorations are old but we love to talk about them as to when and where we got them. The two of us really enjoy Christmas music and love to play Christmas CDs while we make Christmas candy. We always have a lot of packages under our tree although most of them are inexpensive gifts. At eleven o'clock on Christmas Eve we go to our church Carbondale Assembly of God for our candlelight communion service. The service is always so beautiful with great Christmas music. The main thing we enjoy is when our family are all home together and our Christmas socks are all hung by the chimney with care. We started out with the two of us and then Melody and Tommy came along and made four. When Tommy got engaged to Dennette, Melody

Grandma's Stories

made her a stocking to hang with our four which made five, then Melody married Mike making six. Thomas number seven, Maeve number eight, Tyler number nine, Niall number ten, and Brendan's sock making eleven. What a beautiful sight. *See Note.

I love everything about Christmas, shopping, wrapping, decorating, food, and of course Santa, but the main thing to remember and to make sure we never forget is that Christmas is really about the birth of our Savior Jesus Christ.

Merry Christmas to all and to all a good night.
December 25, 2001

Note: Celebrating Christmas 2016.

With 17 Stockings! Lauren, Danielle, Brooke, Ardern, Baby Luke

CHRISTMAS TREES

When I was a little girl my mother and I always had a Douglas Fir tree for our Christmas tree. My husband always called a fir tree a "Charlie Brown Tree," because they were skinny and didn't have enough branches. A fir tree was the only tree I thought was a <u>real</u> Christmas tree. Our tree was decorated with a string of lights that were objects such as a Santa, house, or snowman, and always had to have a star on top. Our tree had perfectly hung icicles, made of tin foil which according to my mother had to be hung one at a time and straight down on each side of the branch.

Grandma's Stories

There was no throwing of icicles on my mother's tree. I still have the burned out bulbs which we hang on our tree as decorations.

Our First Christmas Tree

On our first Christmas my husband gave in to me and we bought a real Christmas tree, although he didn't really like it. On our second Christmas we went to a Christmas tree lot and bought a Scotch Pine tree. We had to look each tree over to make sure we got just the right one. Almost every year when we went looking for our tree we would freeze as it was so cold. Melody and Tommy always helped pick out our tree until they left home. At one time our tree had bubble lights, but we really like the more traditional lights and decorations better.

One year we went out into the woods with our next door neighbors Billie and Delbert Rahe and their daughter Kaye. Delbert and my husband each cut a Red Cedar tree, which we tied on top of our Rambler station wagon. Our neighbors where such great people and we had so much fun together.

Mom Saulmon's Silver Tree

There was one year my mother-in-law just had to have one of those u̲g̲l̲y̲ silver trees. Do you remember the tree with the color wheel? The wheel turned around and made the tree change colors from red, to green, to blue. That tree didn't last very many years.

For about two years we went down by Kellyville to a Christmas tree farm and picked out our tree to cut. The people who owned the farm provided saws and would help you cut and load your tree. While looking for the perfect tree they gave us hot chocolate to drink. We really enjoyed getting our tree there, but after a couple of years we went back to buying the Scotch Pine trees at the Christmas tree lot. We bought a Scotch Pine tree for many years.

One year we all went to Melody and Mike's for Christmas and they decided to get a large tree. The tree was put in their foyer and was so large they had to tie ropes on the tree and get on the second floor landing to raise it up. The tree was taller than the railing on the second floor landing. The tree was gorgeous, but they said never again.

Last year my husband decided we should get an artificial tree because he believes real trees dry out so fast with the fire place burning that they could start a fire. I did not want to get one because I like the mess and smell of a real tree. I will have to admit that our tree is beautiful. What makes a tree beautiful are all the decorations you put on it. The memories of each item you put on the tree is what makes your tree special. Each year our tree has had Peppermint Candy Canes for our children and now our grandchildren. Sometimes our friends have been known to get one. We have a collection of decorations including some made by our children, grandchildren, and my husband's sister Jeri. We have every color and style imaginable, each with its own story.

Our nativity set my husband made our first Christmas has been under our tree each year along with a star on the top of our tree. The nativity and star are there to remind us of the birth of Jesus. MERRY CHRISTMAS TO ALL!

December 2001

TULSA GOSPELAIRES

When I was a teenager I played the piano for the Tulsa Gospelaires Quartet. The quartet was comprised of Johnny DeWeese tenor, Bill Martin lead, H. R. McCartney baritone, and Howard Gwartney bass. These four men had to be the greatest guys in the world. I consider them to be among my very best friends.

Grandma's Stories

Howard, Johnny, and Bill wanted to start a quartet, but they needed the fourth person. I believe Howard lived in Berryhill next door to H. R. and knew he could sing. Howard invited H. R. to sing with them and thus the beginning of the Tulsa Gospelaires. I considered myself very blessed to have been asked to play the piano for them.

Tulsa Gospelaires: Me, Howard, H. R., Bill, Johnny

The quartet sang for churches, singing convention, etc. The big thrill came when they got to sing at the Old Lady of Brady, which at that time was the Tulsa Convention Center. This was the Big Time!

All of us except H. R. went to Lawnwood Free Will Baptist Church. H. R. went to the West Tulsa Nazarene Church. Once in a while we would talk H. R. into going to church with us so they could sing there. Our Pastor Gene Winfrey didn't like it when we went to sing at other churches as it took "his" piano player and "his" quartet.

When we practiced we would either go to H. R.'s house or my house. Many times when we practiced at H. R.'s, his mother Mrs. Alta McCartney would make us a chocolate mayonnaise cake, the cake would be delicious! Mrs. McCartney was such a sweet lady. I will never forget the time Johnny walked up to the door and said, "I smell a chocolate mayonnaise cake." When we were through practicing sure enough there was that beautiful cake. (I have Mrs. McCartney's recipe and make her cake quite often.)

Our quartet had a radio broadcast on Saturday afternoon from Pryor, Oklahoma. The call letters were KOLS 1570 on the dial. The station was owned by Mr. L. L. Gaffney. The cost of the broadcast was either fifty cents or one dollar a minute. The listeners would send in donations to help pay for the broadcast. Our theme song was I'm Satisfied with Jesus. When the

Grandma's Stories

quartet sang they stood around an RCA ZZDX microphone. There was no such thing as everyone having their own mike.

One Saturday there was a mix up as to who would pick me up for the broadcast. I was left behind and heartbroken. I was sure I had been replaced. The first thing Howard said when they came on the air was "they were sorry for the mix up and that they would be after me in time for our Saturday night appointment." I was the happiest girl in town.

Sometimes after the broadcast we would go to Jess and Tishia Gwartney's farm at Rose, Oklahoma. Mr. and Mrs. Gwartney were Howard's parents. We would spend the night with the Gwartney's and then sing at some church in that area on Sunday morning. Mr. and Mrs. Gwartney were such great people, we really loved them. Mrs. Gwartney would always cook us a country breakfast of bacon, sausage, eggs, biscuits and gravy. The breakfast was delicious. Nelda Gwartney, Howard's wife, was our number one fan. We all loved and appreciated her.

The quartet made a record with a lot of help from Mr. Gaffney. We recorded two songs on a big black 78 rpm. The two songs were Roll On Jordan, which at that time was one of the most popular quartet songs. The other song was I Love the Lord, written by Howard. Whenever I talk to anyone about the quartet almost everyone says "I remember that beautiful song, I Love the Lord."

Mr. Gaffney made a tape of the two songs and sent them to Gospel Records of Fresno, California who produced the record. Mr. Gaffney also secured us permission to record Roll On Jordan. The day we recorded the tape for the record, the pedal on the piano was broken which didn't do anything to help the sound of the piano. After all these years, my record is one of my prized possessions.

Howard was drafted into the Army and left January 12, 1953. This was the breakup of the Tulsa Gospelaires. I made some great friends from the members of the quartet. I will never forget the members and all the good times we had together. After the breakup of our quartet everyone went their own separate way. Johnny and H. R. joined the Army, Bill got married and worked for DX Sunray, and I finished high school. Bill and his wife Myra Lee had two children, a boy and a girl. Bill passed away December 12, 1981. Myra Lee remarried and her last name is now Underwood. Johnny DeWeese lived in Arlington, Texas with his wife and I believe three children. Sometime in the late 1960s Johnny, his wife, and children were all involved in a car wreck which killed his wife and children. Johnny died May 30, 1994. H. R. lives with his wife Elsie in Vacaville, California. The McCartneys have two daughters and three grandchildren. H. R. was a civilian working for the Navy as a Ship Surveyor at the time of his retirement. Howard and Nelda live in Locust Grove, Oklahoma. The Gwartneys have three sons and nine grandchildren. Howard is a Missionary Builder for the Free Will Baptists. Howard and Nelda travel all over the country building churches. My husband C. R. Layton and I have a daughter and a son, also the world's five greatest grandchildren. My husband retired from American Airlines. We live in Berryhill in the house that we had Howard build forty years ago. I have had a great life being a wife, mom, and grandmother. Thanks to the members of the Tulsa Gospelaires for much of my happiness.

THE WATERMELON STAND

The Watermelon Stand was located on the southeast corner of Fourth and Denver in downtown Tulsa, Oklahoma. This was a place where you could sit and eat a slice of watermelon. I believe it was 25 cents a slice. The people who owned the stand had a really large, crude box full of ice water the melons were kept in and they were really cold. The tables and chairs were not much to be desired but they gave you a place to sit while you enjoyed your watermelon.

When I was little Mom and I would ride the streetcar to Denver, get off and walk to Fourth Street. Somewhere along the way we had to walk by the only home there. The people who lived there were Mexicans. I found out later in life that they were a very large noisy family named Zunica. They would talk so loud and of course you couldn't understand a word they said and I was really afraid of them. I found out much later that Connie was a friend of Joe Zunica and played football with him in Junior High School.

After Connie and I were married we would go to the stand. We lived just a few blocks from there at Seventh and Lansing. After a while I found out I was pregnant with Melody Joy. Well you know pregnant women have cravings and have to have something special and mine was watermelon. Being the loving husband he was he took me to get a piece in our 1957 Ford. We could not find a parking place anywhere, but Connie spotted a place right on the corner across the street from the watermelon stand but it was right in front of a fireplug. When we came back to get in our car guess who was there. That's right, a policeman writing us a ticket. Connie told him he was sorry but that was the only place to park and being pregnant I had to have my watermelon. The policeman looked at me and saw me as big as a barrel and tore up the ticket.

THE WAY AND TIME I MET MY HUSBAND

I had a friend whose name was Geraldine McClain, known to me as Jeri, who was my husband's sister. Jeri had told the young ladies at our church about her little brother, Connie (his real name is Conrad), who was a lonesome airman in Alaska and asked us to write to him. I wrote to him and he wrote back to me; we wrote to each other several times before he came home.

It just so happened that I found out he would be coming home the night of November 22, 1955. That night I made it a point to go to his parents', Ivy and Lucille Saulmon's, house at 5935 W. 8th St., Tulsa, Oklahoma to use their encyclopedia books that I really needed. Low and behold, in walked this handsome, blonde haired, hazel eyed guy I had been writing to. He was even better looking than I had imagined, although he had a handlebar

Grandma's Stories

mustache which I don't remember being crazy about. The mustache didn't last long.

I don't know if he knew what I was thinking when I saw him, but I said to myself I was going to get a date with him before the other girls had a chance. Connie took me home that night, told me he would call me soon and we would get together. Connie called me the next day and asked me out. I told him our church was having Thanksgiving services the next day and he could take me if he wanted to. We went to church that Thanksgiving November 24, 1955. This date was the beginning of our romance. I felt as I had known him forever.

That chance meeting led to our marriage January 11, 1957, at Crusaders Temple. Our marriage was 42 years ago and he is still the man of my dreams, and the love of my life. I also gained a sister, Jeri.

Jimmy Doyle Woods, C.R, me, Peggy Emigh,
Pastor Gene Winfrey

EXPECTING OUR FIRST CHILD

The first year after my husband and I were married, I found out that I was pregnant. My husband and I were young; I was 19 and my husband was 23. Everything seemed to be going so well, and we were thrilled. We felt like we were the only couple to ever have a baby, or at least our baby would be the greatest child ever.

"What a difference a day makes." Everything went from going well to everything going wrong. On a day in June 1957 I began to bleed, and called my doctor, Dr. William McShane. My husband took me to St. Johns Hospital in Tulsa, Oklahoma as instructed. After being admitted, I was taken to my room. Shortly thereafter, two doctors that I believe were interns came into my room and told me I would have to go to surgery. I told the doctors that I wasn't going anywhere until my own doctor told me our baby was dead. No one will ever know how I felt.

Scared and heartbroken, I don't believe I had realized how much I really wanted our baby until then. I prayed so many times that day. I bought a newspaper to have something to read and when I picked it up, there staring me in the face was the Bible verse which read "according to your faith, so shall it be." (Matthew 9:29) At that time, I knew everything would be okay. That afternoon, Dr. McShane came to see me with a smile on his face. He told me everything would be fine, that our baby was just as alive as any baby had ever had been. We were so very thankful to God.

Being careful for the next six months was hard, but we all made it. On Christmas Day 1957, our beautiful daughter was born. What a great Christmas present! Our daughter was healthy, and had a lot of long black hair. We named our daughter Melody Joy. Melody has been one of the greatest Joys of our lives, just like a beautiful piece of music.

THIS OLD HOUSE

Shortly after my husband and I were married in 1957 we decided we wanted to own our own home. We started looking at houses in all areas of town. After looking around for a while we decided we would like to find a lot and build our own home. I had some friends who lived in Berryhill and I liked the area. One day when we were out looking we decided to drive to Berryhill and really look. We drove by the school and football field which helped us decide that this was the place. We are still glad we chose to build our home in Berryhill.

Our Pastor Gene Winfrey had an acre he wanted to sell. Gene made us an offer of $1400 and I talked him down to $1350. (I'm a big bargain hunter.) When we bought the acre it was being used as a horse pasture and practice field by high school football players. Almost every night during the two years we were paying for our lot we would drive over to see if our

Grandma's Stories

land was still there. Sure enough there it was just like we left it the night before.

The night we paid off the loan we took my husband's Mother and Dad, my Mother and Uncle John, and our daughter Melody out to our favorite place to eat. We went to Pancho's on 11th St. for dinner and a celebration.

Soon we contracted our friend Howard Gwartney who helped us decide what we could afford and how much money we would need to build our house. We had two cars which we sold. One car was a 1957 Ford Fairlane 500 and the other one was a 1954 Ford Deluxe. We bought a 1948 Chrysler New Yorker which became our limo. We applied for and were granted a loan. We were now on our way to build our dream home. Our payments were $67.00 including tax and insurance.

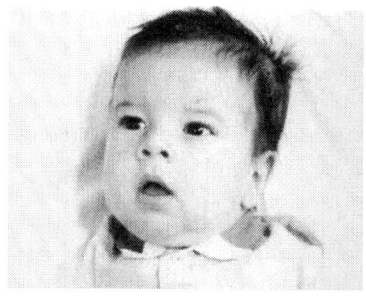

Tommy

My husband and I hired Howard to rough in the house. Most of the work was done by us, but we hired a few things done. We had our neighbor Charles Hinesley put in the septic system. A friend of ours Charles "Scrubby" Lovelace was hired to hang the sheetrock. We did most of the finish work of roofing, painting, and finishing cabinets, etc. We spent almost every evening and weekend working on our house. I was pregnant and as big as a barrel, but I would sit on the floor and work on the kitchen cabinets. I don't know how in the world I ever got up.

One day my husband came over and found the tile man in the bathtub as "drunk as a skunk" as they used to say. The man was singing at the top of his lungs and was sticking tile here and there on the wall. The poor guy was putting tile everywhere except where he was supposed to. My husband went across the street and called the tile company to tell them they had better come after their drunk Indian! The tile company sent someone after their man, and sent two men to undo and redo his mess. Our house was

Grandma's Stories

finished just about like it is now except the porch and den have been enlarged and a fireplace and patio added.

While we were building, Okla Mouser the lady across the street would come over and mow, so Melody would have a place to play. Once in a while Okla would bring us great strawberry malts. She was a great lady and we really miss her.

C.R. with Tommy and Melody

On Saturday I would usually come over and bring my husband lunch. Sometimes I would find him and his friend Bill Sasser pitching horse shoes, but they worked very hard. The second week of August 1960 we moved in our house. Melody was two and a half, and Tommy was a week and a half. My husband and our brother-in-law brought me, Melody, and Tommy over to the house and left us while they moved us in. Moving us in wasn't much work considering what we had to move. We had two metal folding tables we used for end tables, and two lawn chairs. We had a baby bed Melody still slept in and a bassinet for Tommy. We had a piano, guitar, cedar chest, dining room table and chairs. We bought a cheap dark brown living room suite, which was a sofa bed with the two humps. The sofa was our bed by night and when folded in the morning it became our sofa. This was a great piece of furniture, two in one! We were so happy with our children and our dream home it didn't matter the we didn't have it all. Our house at S. 63rd W. Ave. was our dream home. The mailing address for our house is Tulsa, Oklahoma, but, it is in the community of Berryhill.

Later when our children were about twelve and fourteen, they told us what they wanted for Christmas. The children were tired of off white walls and beige carpet in their rooms. For Christmas that year they asked us if we would allow them to decorate their rooms like they wanted them. Well, guess what? We told them they could and they became "decorators." Melody wanted blue walls, blue shag carpet, and white curtains. Melody found a pretty spread with blue flowers. Tom, on the other hand, was a little more daring. Tommy picked out bright orange paint, orange and gold shag carpet, and bright green curtains, and matching spread. When you entered Tom's room it felt light a great big light had just been turned on. Both of the kids loved their rooms and if that small thing made them happy it was fine with mom and daddy.

The den was enlarged by C. R. and Tommy. Most all the lumber and rock came from houses that the city had torn down to build the Broken Arrow Expressway. We would haul in rock from anywhere a building was being torn down. The rock was getting hard to find and very expensive. We had noticed an insurance company building, at Thirteenth and Cheyenne that was to be auctioned and moved. Everything had to go including a very large flower bed in front of the building. The flower bed had a lot of rock and ledge stone, which we really needed. On the day of the auction my husband had to work so you can guess who went to the auction. I got a friend of mine to go with me for moral support. Before the auction started I told the auctioneer what I was there for and that I didn't have a clue as to what I was supposed to do. The auctioneer was very nice and told me to stand by him and when the flower bed came up for bid to say, "I'll give one dollar." As soon as I said one dollar the man said, "sold to the little lady." I just imagine that everyone there was wondering what the little lady was going to do with that flower bed. I came home very proud of myself. Of course we had to tear the flower bed apart and haul it home rock by rock. When we were enlarging the den, Melody's beagle dog Berryhill Chief would steal any tool, glove, or anything he could carry off. Chief would go hide it and watch you look for it. After a while he would give you a big doggie smile and then he would go look at it. Chief wouldn't bring it back, but he would show you where he put it.

Grandma's Stories

The patio was later added with flat rock my husband hauled home from his hunting and fishing outings. C. R. collected every pretty flat rock he thought would look good.

We paid our house off early simply because I wanted that paid in full paper! For a man who had never built a house before or laid a rock I believe he did a great job. I will always love him for being such a wonderful husband and dad, and always providing so well for us. Our home will be forty-one years old in August of this year, 2001. The memories that we have of our home will always be treasured. Our home has always been a place of fun, food, family, and friends.

March 2001

RAISING OUR CHILDREN

When I was a young girl about nine years old, I became friends with a girl just about my age, Jean Marie Wooldridge. I believe we meet thru our piano teacher, Mr. R. B. Condry. We both went to "singing schools" taught by Mr. R. B. Condry, where we were taught to read shape notes, sing harmony, direct a choir, and learned about the theory of music.

During the summer we went to the Free Will Baptist Youth Camp held at the Free Will Baptist camp grounds in Drumright, Oklahoma. We had some great times there. After we got a little older we lost contact with each other. Some years later Jean Marie met and married her husband Charles "Chuck" Rogers. I married my husband January 11, 1957 and shortly after our marriage we bought a lot and started making plans to build our dream home in Berryhill. We built our home and moved in August of 1960.

Me and C.R., Tommy and Melody

About two years after we moved into our home the Rogers' family bought a house on the same street we live on not knowing who would be their neighbors. Chuck and Jean Marie have 5 children: LaCresha, Alan, Bricky, Wesley, and Lance. My husband and I along

Grandma's Stories

with our children, Melody and Tommy, soon became good friends with the Rogers' family. We raised our kids along with the other kids on our block. From one corner of the block to the other there were 21 children. On Saturday nights Chuck and Jean Marie, my husband and I played Canasta while the kids played together. The guys went fishing or frog hunting sometimes staying all night. A lot of the time us girls and the children would load up a car and show up the next morning wherever the guys were fishing. We cooked many a big breakfast on the creek bank. Jean Marie makes the <u>blackest, strongest, awful</u> coffee you can imagine, "Creek Coffee." She thinks it's wonderful. I just close my eyes and down it. I guess when it's all you have it's OK.

There were days when we would take all 7 of our children to the T.G.Y. store in Crystal City Shopping Center. We would just walk up and down the aisles looking as we did not have much spending money. The kids were wonderful about not asking for anything, they already knew there was not much money.

In Red Fork on S.W. Blvd. there was a store owned by Mr. and Mrs. Hopkins called Hopkins Variety. On one side of the store were the things for ladies, and on the other side was the fix it stuff, such as plumbing and electrical supplies. Mrs. Hopkins knew a lot of the ladies didn't have much extra spending money so she had the Hopkins Layaway plan. If a lady came in wanting several skeins of yarn with the same die lot she would say, "Why don't you just take one skein today and I will put the rest in a box with your name on it, and when you want another one come back and get it." I would say this was a Mrs. Hopkins special layaway plan.

On Tuesdays we ironed all day. Most of the time I took my ironing to Jean Marie's house as she had a lot more to iron than I did, but sometimes she came to my house. We would iron until noon, then we would have lunch which was usually a sandwich, chips, pop, etc.

After lunch it was more of the same, ironing until about three o'clock. The children would play all day while we ironed, watched the soaps, talked, and probably gossiped just a little.

Grandma's Stories

When the kids started to school we became Homeroom Mothers. Each class had two Homeroom Mothers who were chosen by the teacher. We ended up being Homeroom Mothers together several years. One of our jobs was to make P.T.A. announcements each month and go to school and pin them on the children's clothing so they would not lose them on the way home. All that was required for us to do was cut out a square of paper and write the message: please come to P.T.A. tonight at 7:30. The square message was not good enough for us, we always made something to go with the month. One Halloween we made skeletons which had arms and legs that moved up and down. This was our way of having fun. For class parties Jean Marie and I made <u>special</u> cupcakes and cookies decorated for the holiday we were celebrating. Nothing too good for <u>OUR KIDS</u>.

LaCresha and Melody were best friends and belonged to Campfire Girls. The night of the Father and Daughter Banquet the girls picked out their dad's ties to wear and were so proud of how handsome their dads looked. Melody's dad's tie was orange and purple.

We all attended New Home Free Will Baptist Church in Berryhill for years and all the kids accepted Christ and were baptized in that church except Lance who was too young when they changed churches.

We did serious things for each other as well, such as taking children to the doctor, babysitting, etc. One time I remember Jean Marie took me to the nursing home in Sapulpa where my mother lived. The people at the Salvation Army in Sapulpa were so good to my mother, they always came and took her to church, and when they had something special they always came after her. On this particular day they were having a dinner and Mom had told them, "I'll bring a pie," which meant "Beverly will make a pie for me to bring" which was fine only I had no way to get it there. Mom could have gone without it but it made her feel much better to have something to contribute. All I had to do was tell Jean Marie my plight and off we went kids, pie and all! I don't believe she knows how important that was to me or my mother.

This is what friendship is all about--being ready to help in any situation. We could always count on each other. Now the children are all grown up, self-sufficient, and live all over the country. My husband and I, Chuck and Jean Marie still live in the same two houses, are still friends, and now play Mexican Train Dominoes together.
July 2004

HOME ROOM MOTHERS

Homeroom Mothers were a group of women at Berryhill Grade School who the teachers would select at the beginning of each year to help them with little social jobs that would make school more fun. The rule was that you could only be a Homeroom Mother every other year for each child you had in school.

A lot of mothers really wanted to be chosen for this very lofty job. I was fortunate enough to be chosen every year. The first year for our daughter and the next year for our son. I still remember our teachers, Mrs. Lee, Mrs. Hargis, and Mrs. Jamison. This was a fun job, we did little jobs to help out our teacher, and we planned and held parties for the children on Valentines, Easter, and Halloween. Each month we made reminders for PTA meetings, which we would pin on the children's clothing for their parents to see when they got home from school.

Each month the mothers got together for a luncheon and we had a lady who was our overseer and director. It was her job to tell each mother what to bring for their next luncheon and when it was all put together it always turned out to be a very fine meal.

I remember one year Betty McCartney was our leader. Betty was a really good cook and famous for her culinary arts and ability. She would enter her famous pies and cakes and anything else in the Tulsa State Fair that she thought would win the blue ribbon. Her wonderful pecan pie was always the winner. She would always come home with the Blue Ribbons.

Grandma's Stories

One month for our monthly luncheon she was compelled to ask me to make a pecan pie. At first I thought it was just trying to show me up as I had never made a pecan pie in my life. I was really worried, but guess what? My pie was delicious. Betty is a lovely lady and it was happenstance that I got the job of pecan pie making.

Another year Laura Belle Geiger was our leader. At the end of the year she took the entire group of Homeroom Mothers to a wonderful restaurant at 31st and Harvard called Conner's Corner for lunch and then to see "The Sound of Music" which had just been released. Laura Belle paid for it all. I just could not believe anyone would pay out that much money for anything like this. But this was her way of thanking the ladies for a job well done.

Now for the most important part of our job. I had a best friend who happened to be a Homeroom Mother at the same time I was. The lady was Jean Marie Rogers and we did everything together. I guess some would say we tried to outdo all the others but that was not true. It just happened to work out that way! Each month when we would make PTA reminders ours were a little fancier than the other classes. When we got to school the other mothers would have a small square piece of construction paper saying "PTA tonight 7:30." But not us, one year we made jack o' lanterns. Every month we did something special that was holiday or school oriented, but one year was the topper, we made skeletons with moving arms and legs. Only the best for us!

A CHILD'S FAITH

For our vacation in about the year 1968 we planned on a trip to Missouri. We loaded in our 1962 red and white Rambler Classic and started on our trip. Our daughter Melody was about ten years old, and our son Tommy was eight. Our plans included a trip to Jefferson City, which is the capitol of Missouri. Melody was intrigued with capitol buildings, every state we visited had to include a trip to their capitol building. Our son

Grandma's Stories

Tommy tolerated the capitol visits only because he knew he would get to do what he wanted to do.

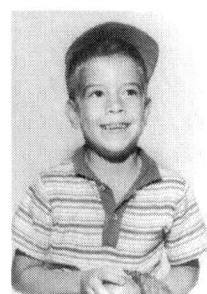

Tommy

The main attraction on the agenda that year was a trip to Busch Stadium, home of the St. Louis Cardinals Major League Baseball Team. None of us had ever been to a Major League game and we were all looking forward to it. The ball game was all Tommy talked about for days before we left. Everyone Tommy talked to had to hear that we were going to St. Louis, Missouri to see the Cardinals play a ball game. The Cardinals were Tommy's favorite team then and now.

We were staying at a Sheraton Hotel about three miles from the stadium. The night before the game it started raining "cats and dogs." The day of the game we got up and sure enough it was pouring down. We hated to tell Tommy that there was no chance of a ball game and that we would not be going to the ball park. Tommy was heartbroken and began to cry. We were told in no uncertain terms that "we were going to the stadium and there would be a game." Since we were only about three miles from the park we gave in and started for the stadium in the rain. It rained on us until about six blocks from Busch Stadium. When we got to this point the ground was as dry as a bone and not a drop of rain had fallen on the field. Tommy simply replied, "I told you it wouldn't rain on the field, I prayed all night." What an answer to an eight year old boy's prayer. As the Bible says, "according to your Faith so shall it be."

We saw a great game between the San Francisco Giants and Cardinals with Juan Marichal pitching the game for the Giants and Bob Gibson pitching for the Cardinals. The Cardinals won which made the game perfect. Bob Gibson was Tommy's idol at the time. A good time was had by all.

July 20, 2001

Made in the USA
Middletown, DE
21 May 2017